Δόξα Πατρί και Υιώ και Αγίω Πνεύματι. Και νυν και αεί και εις τους αιώνας των αιώνων. Αμήν.

TABLE OF CONTENTS

Design is the bridge that connects the realms of imagination and reality, transforming dreams into tangible expressions of our innermost desires.

- Katerina Kapellaki

A WORD FROM THE AUTHOR

Beautiful people, I extend my warmest welcome to you, esteemed connoisseurs of refinement and sophistication. Your presence here is truly a delight, and I am genuinely thrilled to have you here with me. Really, I am !!!

As we embark on this opulent journey, your presence here is not merely appreciated—it's celebrated. I am Katerina Kapellaki, your guide into a realm where design transcends the ordinary, and luxury finds its truest form. This is your invitation to an elite gathering of global design luminaries, an exclusive backstage pass to the grand spectacle of interior design and architecture and the alchemical transformation of spaces, touches the very essence of our existence. It weaves through the tapestry of our homes, workplaces, sanctuaries, and indulgent retreats. Its purpose: to elevate functionality, infuse beauty, and craft an ambiance that whispers opulence. As connoisseurs of interiors and architecture, your mission is to orchestrate harmony, crafting spaces that inspire awe and admiration.

Within these pages, you'll discover a flavor, a zest, and a style that will make understanding interior design an enchanting voyage. Just like you, I view design as a gift, a privilege that empowers us to fashion spaces that are not only opulent but also eminently functional. In the chapters that follow, I will do more than just explain this perspective; I will immerse you in a world where excellence and extravagance are the norm.

As we delve into the enchanting realm of Design Decadence A–Ω. I am excited to introduce you to some of my meticulously selected connections within the world of interior design, architecture and construction. Their wisdom and talents will illuminate the path we tread, enriching your journey through the opulent world of this global high-end coffee table book. So, let us embark on this exquisite adventure, where opulence and inspiration know no bounds.

> Step into my world, or let me step into yours and I'll introduce you to a bit of decadence, my artform.
>
> - Katerina Kapellaki

Interior design is an art form that ignites inspiration through walls, light, and ideas. It transcends words, speaking volumes through its visual language. Beyond furniture and colors, it breathes life into spaces, transforming them into realms of inspiration.

With a focus on making a difference, we integrate social change into our business model, tying each profit experience to a non-profit initiative. Passion and giving back drive our purpose. Inspired by my upbringing, Greek ancient architecture, and my family, my mission is to create stunning spaces that leave a lasting impact, one room at a time.

ANCIENT MINOAN ARCHITECTURE AND KNOSSOS PALACE

WHERE IT ALL BEGAN

My Architectural inspiration comes from my island home of Crete, Greece. Crete, with its rich history and the ancient Minoan civilization, offers a treasure trove of architectural wonders that have stood the test of time. Drawing inspiration from my home island's heritage which infuse my designs with a unique blend of history, culture, and innovation. Minoan architecture often embraced the surrounding landscape and incorporated natural elements. Emulating this connection to nature in your designs can create harmonious spaces that blend seamlessly with their environment.

The Minoans using sustainable building practices relied on locally sourced materials and environmentally friendly construction methods. Integrating sustainable building practices into your designs can pay homage to the ancient civilization while promoting eco-consciousness.

Minoan buildings were designed to optimize natural light and ventilation. Their ancient architecture displayed a sense of fluidity and organic forms. Integrating curves and soft lines in your designs can create a sense of movement and elegance.

09

The Minoan civilization, which flourished on the island of Crete, Greece during the Bronze Age (Atleast 8000 years ago), is renowned for its sophisticated architecture and advanced urban planning. One of the most significant architectural marvels of the Minoan civilization is the Knossos Palace, located near the modern city of Heraklion in Crete. The palace at Knossos is not only an extraordinary architectural achievement but also provides valuable insights into the social, cultural, and religious aspects of Minoan society.

The Knossos Palace complex covers an area of approximately 20,000 square meters and is believed to have been a multifunctional structure that served as a royal residence, administrative center, and religious sanctuary. Its layout features a series of interconnected courtyards, corridors, and rooms that were organized around a central courtyard. The intricate design of the palace demonstrates a high level of urban planning and architectural sophistication.

The Minoans were skilled architects and builders, and their use of limestone, mud bricks, and timber allowed them to create a grand and impressive complex that has fascinated archaeologists, historians, and visitors for centuries.

Today, the ruins of Knossos Palace still stand as a testament to the remarkable engineering and architectural achievements of the Minoan civilization, showcasing the use of locally sourced materials to construct a sophisticated and culturally significant palace complex. They were innovative in their use of multi-story architecture. The Knossos Palace is a prime example of this, as it consists of multiple floors, including a ground floor and upper stories. This design allowed for the optimization of space and facilitated better ventilation and light penetration.

Limestone is a sedimentary rock that is abundant in the region. It is easily quarried and shaped, making it an ideal material for the Minoans to construct their monumental buildings. The palace's walls, columns, and some of its architectural elements were made from limestone blocks.

In addition to limestone, the Minoans also used mud bricks as a construction material. Mud bricks were made from clay, sand, and straw, and they were used to build some of the palace's walls and partitions. For structural support, timber beams and columns were also incorporated into the construction. These wooden elements added strength and stability to the multi-story architecture of Knossos Palace.

The palace was constructed using innovative and advanced construction techniques with locally sourced limestone and mud bricks. Beams and columns provided structural support to the building. The Minoans were adept at using lightweight materials and innovative construction techniques, which allowed them to create spacious, airy interiors.

Knossos palace features grand staircases and well-planned corridors that connected different sections of the complex. These architectural elements not only facilitated movement within the palace but also added to the overall grandeur and magnificence of the structure.

The Minoans distinctive columns and pillars were known for their unique architectural ways, particularly the "Minoan column" or "Cretan column." These columns are characterized by a distinctive bell-shaped capital, tapering shaft, and often fluted design. The columns at Knossos Palace were made of wood or limestone and showcased the Minoan's architectural style.

The walls and decorative art of Knossos Palace were adorned with elaborate frescoes depicting scenes of everyday life, religious rituals, and mythological themes. These vibrant and colorful artworks provided a glimpse into the artistic talent and cultural practices of the Minoans.

The central court and throne room of the palace were significant open spaces surrounded by various rooms and corridors. This area likely served as a public gathering place and might have hosted ceremonies and festivities. The throne room, known as the "Megaron," was a distinguished and elaborately decorated space where the ruler held court and conducted official affairs.

The innovative plumbing and underfloor heating system excites me the most. The Minoans were technologically advanced in their use of water management. Knossos Palace featured an intricate plumbing system with terracotta pipes that transported water to various parts of the complex, including bathrooms and drainage systems. The Minoans of the Bronze Age were known for their advanced engineering and architectural innovations, and the Knossos Palace provides evidence of their sophisticated understanding of heating systems. Excavations at the palace have revealed a remarkable underfloor heating system, demonstrating the Minoans' ingenuity in creating comfortable living spaces.

The underfloor heating system at Knossos Palace was known as a "hypocaust" and was a remarkable feat for its time. It involved a network of clay pipes placed under the floors of various rooms and corridors throughout the palace. These pipes allowed for the circulation of hot air generated by a central hearth or furnace. The Minoans used this system to control the indoor climate, especially during colder months

14

The heat from the hypocaust system rose through the clay pipes, warming the floors and, consequently, the rooms above. This method of heating provided a comfortable and evenly distributed warmth, making the living spaces more pleasant for the palace's inhabitants.

The presence of such an advanced heating system at Knossos Palace showcases the Minoans' engineering prowess and their desire for sophisticated living conditions. The use of underfloor heating not only demonstrates their knowledge of heating principles but also highlights their ability to create efficient and practical solutions to improve the comfort and well-being of their society. The hypocaust system at Knossos Palace remains a fascinating example of early heating technology and a testament to the ingenuity of the Minoan civilization.

Knossos Palace also contained spaces dedicated to religious and ceremonial activities. Shrines, altars, and sanctuaries were distributed throughout the complex, emphasizing the significance of religion and spirituality in Minoan life.

Seismic Architecture is a specialty of the Minoans and now Cretans as Crete is susceptible to earthquakes, and the Minoans designed their buildings to withstand seismic events. The use of lightweight materials and certain architectural features allowed for flexibility and resilience during earthquakes.

The Knossos Palace stands as a remarkable testament to the architectural ingenuity and artistic prowess of the Minoan civilization. Its intricate layout, distinctive columns, decorative frescoes, and advanced construction techniques showcase the sophistication and creativity of this ancient culture. The palace not only served as a political and administrative center but also played a crucial role in shaping the cultural and religious practices of the Minoan people. Today, the ruins of Knossos Palace continue to be a captivating archaeological site, drawing visitors from around the world to marvel at the remnants of this ancient architectural masterpiece.

Κρήτη μου η παράδοση,
Και τα ιστορικά σου,
Αθάνατο εκάμανε στον
Κόσμο τ΄όνομά σου .

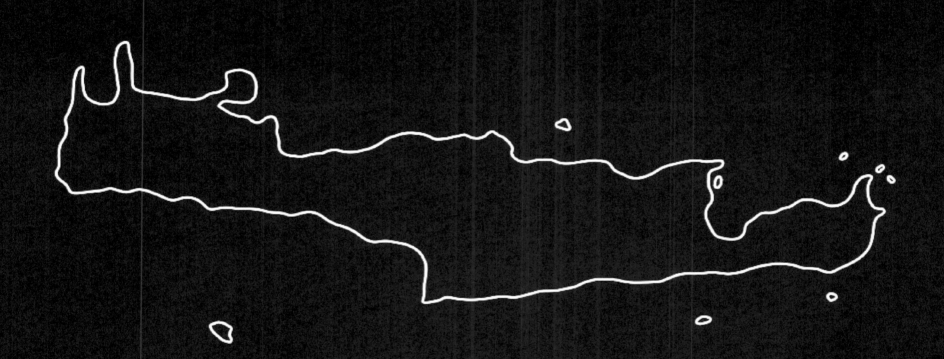

MINIMALIST
INTERIOR DESIGN

THE ELEMENTS OF INTERIOR DESIGN

SPACE

Space is one of the most important elements of interior design. Space acts as a foundation on which the entire interior design plan is built. It is essential that the designer is well aware of the space available, its dimensions, and its utilities. Space is divided into two types namely: two-dimensional space, which covers the floor (includes length and width), and three-dimensional space, which forms the living space (includes length, width and height). A space that is essentially filled with furniture/décor items is known as "positive space" and an empty space is known as "negative space". The goal is to balance the positive and negative spaces and avoid making the space look either crowded or bland.

LINE

Lines give birth to forms and shapes and are responsible for establishing a sense of harmony, contrast and unity in a living space. They define shapes and act as visual guides of an interior space. Lines are broadly categorized into three types: horizontal, vertical and dynamic. While horizontal lines adorn structures like tables, chairs and beds, vertical lines can be found on windows and doorways. While horizontal lines add a safe and secure feeling to the space, vertical lines are free and expansive. Dynamic or angular lines are action oriented and add drama, which can be seen on structures like stairs. It's certainly rewarding to know how to use these lines to define the forms and shapes.

FORM

Forms are generally shapes, which can be seen as an outline of any three dimensional object in the space. Forms can be created by combining two or more shapes. They'll be more noticeable with the help of other elements like texture, patterns and colors. A well-defined form establishes harmony while additional forms add balance to the space. There are two types of forms – geometric (man-made) and natural (organic). Also, forms are categorized as open and closed; open forms are those that can be looked into and closed forms are those that are enclosed by a closed surface. A solid understanding of everything so far will help you achieve a good form.

LIGHT

Lighting is crucial in interior design as it showcases color, texture, and pattern, while also setting the mood and creating ambience. It can be divided into three major types: task lighting, accent lighting, and mood lighting. Task lighting serves a specific purpose and includes fixtures like table and bed lamps. Accent lighting is used to highlight specific elements such as artwork or structures. Mood lighting sets the overall mood of the space and illuminates the entire area. By understanding these types of lighting and utilizing them effectively, you can create a well-lit and visually appealing interior.

COLOR

Colors in interior design create connections and set moods. They should reflect the dweller's psychology. For example, red stimulates appetite in dining rooms, while green brings tranquility to bedrooms. Colors have three characteristics: hue, value, and intensity. Designers must understand these traits to create diverse designs. Colors are classified as primary, secondary, and subcategories like tertiary, complementary, analogous, and monochromatic.

TEXTURE

Texture deals with surfaces. It determines how a typical surface looks and feels. Texture adds depth and interest to a living space and defines the feel and consistency of a surface. There are two types of textures: visual texture, where the texture is only visible, and actual texture, where the texture is both seen and felt. Anything that has to do with textiles, such as a pillow cover, bedspreads, drapes, wall paint, and wallpapers have a texture. Although there must be a dominant texture to define a mood, a contrasting texture must be included to prevent the design from looking unattractive; variety is your friend.

PATTERN

Patterns add excitement and life to interior design and work closely with colors. Patterns tell their own. They add continuity and smooth transitions in a living space. Patterns could be of any shape and still keep their attractiveness through repetition. For example, paisley, a design pattern which takes the shape of a droplet-shaped vegetable, is one of the most commonly used patterns on wall paints, pillow covers, and other decorative surfaces.

SIZE

When it comes to size, we often see things in two ways: big or small. For example, a spacious room in a house may be smaller than an open office space taking up an entire floor of a high rise building, but the room will appear large in relation to an adjacent small powder room.

PROPORTION

Proportion in design concerns the balance between elements like shape, color, and texture. It is often associated with scale, which determines the comparative size of objects and remains fixed. Proportion involves the subjective assessment of an arrangement's harmony. Correct proportions are achieved through the repetition of shapes, colors, and textures, careful lighting control, and the incorporation of style and variety.

SCALE

Scale is a crucial aspect of interior design, determining the relative size and character of objects and spaces. Whether it's furniture or rooms, considering human scale is vital to ensure functionality and practicality. A well-designed interior takes into account the proportions and needs of the individuals using the space. For instance, a kitchen should be tailored to the height of the person who uses it most, ensuring a comfortable and efficient experience. By incorporating scale effectively, interior design becomes both aesthetically pleasing and practical.

BALANCE

Balance is what makes the interior totally Zen. Unbalanced relationships will be seen as discomforting or disturbing while balanced relationships give a feeling of restfulness and comfort. Balance in an interior can be achieved in several ways.

In symmetrical balance, the elements are arranged to mirror each other on each side of an invisible line that divides the space itself. This type symmetry is pretty common and familiar, which is why in design; the symmetrical scheme adds importance to the center to create an effect of restfulness and dignity. Proportion and scale are design principles related to balance. Proportion involves the ratio of elements to each other or the whole, while scale deals with object size. Radial symmetry radiates from a central point, seen in foyers. Asymmetrical balance achieves equilibrium through varying elements. The existing architecture often determines the balance approach. Symmetrical balance is formal and fixed, while asymmetrical balance is casual and flexible.

EMPHASIS

In interior design, emphasizing elements enhances certain areas while maintaining a subdued presence elsewhere. For example, a tall translucent blue vase in a white space captures attention. When creating a design scheme, assess the significance of each element in relation to the overall composition. In spaces with stunning views, prioritize and highlight the outlook to avoid overpowering the visual experience.

HARMONY, UNITY, VARIETY AND CONTRAST

To create harmony in interior design, all elements must relate to each other and the overall theme. This creates a seamless unit, rather than a cluster of unrelated items. Coordinated patterns, textures, colors, and stylistic consistency lead to harmony and unity, but too much symmetry can appear bland.

Variety and contrast act as the "surprise" that prevents "dull" or "boring" to ever appear. It gives the viewer different shapes, textures, colors and details to admire. Contrast makes certain values pop. For instance, a light color will appear even lighter if placed next to a darker color; a large object appears larger if placed next to a smaller object. Contrast and variety are the keys to improving the overall impact of an interior.

"Go Totally Zen and Learn From Nature."

RHYTHM

Rhythm refers to the way objects and furnishings in a space form aesthetic patterns.

The best interior design is often related to the surrounding natural environment, especially if the interior has an outlook that celebrates the beauty of a garden, a forest setting, or water view. I've known designers who were working on a color scheme for a building in a forest setting that have explored the local forests and collected samples of the barks and leaves of trees near the area then used these to develop a scheme wonderfully harmonized with the environment.

WORLD OF COLORS

Color palettes are what create trends. Nothing is more personal than color. Choosing a color palette is both important and daunting when it comes to styling homes. Read on and get some great tips as we help guide you to create the color palette that best suits your style, personality and lifestyle.

CHOOSING YOUR COLORS

Start by working from a colour wheel. There are primary, secondary and tertiary colors.

- Primary colors are red, blue and yellow. They are pure colors and cannot be created.

- Secondary colors are orange, green and purple. These colors are formed when equal parts of 2 primary colors are combined. For example equal parts yellow and blue make green. It's basic, but this is where we begin the colour selection.

- Tertiary colors are a mixture in varying parts of secondary and primary colors to create different hues. As a result, the primary and secondary colors become less vivid. White and black are often added to darken and soften these hues.

CREATING YOUR COLOR SCHEME

Use your color wheel to help you create your own color scheme that best fit your personality. There are 4 kinds of possible color schemes.

MONOCHROMATIC

Use tone-on-tone technique with the same color layered. Add white or black to lighten or darken the color. Example: Blue can range from pale sky blue to dark midnight blue. Utilize different hues of the same shade for the desired effect.

ANALOGOUS

Colors adjacent to each other on the color wheel, such as yellow with green or orange, are used together to create a harmonious and soothing color palette.

CONTRAST

A triad of contrasting colors, such as yellow-orange, green-blue, and red-purple, are used together to create a bold and vibrant color palette.

COMPLEMENTARY

Use opposing colors, like blue and orange, to create a bold and energetic color scheme. Start by selecting harder-to-find items such as furniture and rugs before choosing the wall color. Once you have chosen your furniture, you can then proceed to select the wall color, as wall paints can be created in any color and hue.

THINGS TO CONSIDER

When selecting a color palette, consider starting with contrasting elements, combining dark and light shades. To infuse energy into your space, consider incorporating bright accents. If you prefer pale walls, introduce color through furniture, accessories, and rugs. Ensure that bold colors are vibrant and crisp. For a more subtle and softer style, explore neutral shades.

COLOR TONES

Ready to begin? Test colors with paint swatches and fabrics. Draw room plans and sketch in colors. If they work on paper, try painting small wall areas. Buy sample-sized paint. Observe how rooms connect. Create flow from room to room. Adjoining rooms may need non-accent or neutral colors. Work with contrasting tones while maintaining flow.

COLOR FOR CHILDREN

Children generally have specific color preferences which should be incorporated into the design of their bedrooms, childcare centers or childcare wards in hospitals. Children often spend more time in their bedrooms than adults do — entertaining friends, pursuing hobbies and doing their homework. It's their space; they need to feel happy there.

Some suggested schemes would be:

BIRTH TO TWO YEARS

Soft, warm colors such as a mixture of pinks and greens in opaque tints to avoid reflections that might tire a newborn's eyes.

TWO TO FOUR YEARS

Toddlers and small children love bright colors and are attracted to multi- colored, primary hues.

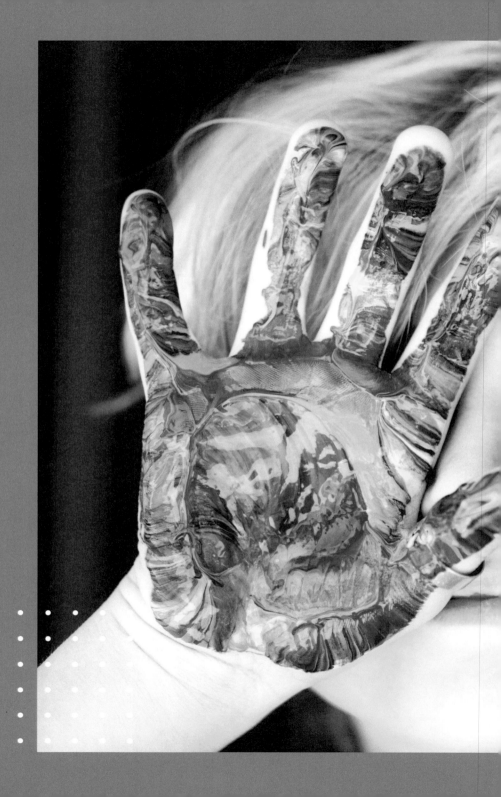

SIX TO 12 YEARS

A neutral background is good for children at this stage, against which they can add colorful accessories and images of their choosing.

TEENAGERS

Teenagers should be allowed to express their own developing taste in their bedrooms but it wouldn't hurt to consult them on the color scheme they choose. For example, you could point out that the bright purple they have chosen for the walls may be a little stimulating and distracting when they are studying for exams!

LE CHIC DETALLE BOHEMIAM FLAME B

KITCHEN DESIGN 101

Kitchen layouts play a crucial role in determining the efficiency and functionality of the space. They are designed to accommodate various cooking tasks, storage needs, and traffic flow. When choosing and designing a kitchen layout, consider the available space, your cooking habits, and the desired level of interaction with family and guests. Each design type offers unique advantages and can be adapted to suit your or your clients specific needs and preferences.

GALLEY KITCHEN

The galley kitchen, also known as a corridor or parallel kitchen, features two parallel countertops with a walkway in between. This layout maximizes efficiency and is ideal for smaller spaces. It provides ample storage and workspace, and the close proximity of appliances makes cooking convenient.

L-SHAPED KITCHEN

The L-shaped kitchen has two adjacent walls forming an "L" configuration. This layout offers a good balance between open space and storage. It provides ample counter space and flexibility in arranging appliances and workstations.

U-SHAPED KITCHEN

The U-shaped kitchen features three walls of cabinets and appliances, forming a "U" shape. This design provides plenty of storage and counter space, making it suitable for large families or avid cooks. It also allows for efficient workflow with distinct zones for preparation, cooking, and cleanup.

ISLAND KITCHEN

The island kitchen incorporates a freestanding workspace or countertop in the center of the kitchen. Islands can be added to various layouts, such as L-shaped or U-shaped, to create additional prep space, storage, and seating. They also serve as a focal point and gathering spot for socializing.

PENINSULA KITCHEN

The peninsula kitchen is an extension of the L-shaped or U-shaped layout, with a connected countertop extending from one of the walls. This design provides extra workspace and serves as a partial room divider, creating an open-concept feel.

ONE-WALL KITCHEN

The one-wall kitchen is characterized by all appliances, cabinets, and countertops aligned on a single wall. This layout is common in studio apartments or small spaces. It maximizes floor space but may offer limited storage and workspace.

OPEN CONCEPT KITCHEN

Open concept kitchens are integrated with other living spaces, such as dining rooms or living rooms, without walls separating them. This layout fosters a sense of openness, allowing for easy interaction and communication between family members and guests.

KITCHEN WITH DINING NOOK

In this layout, the kitchen incorporates a dedicated dining nook or breakfast area. This design provides a cozy space for casual meals and family gatherings.

G-SHAPED KITCHEN

The G-shaped kitchen is an extension of the U-shaped layout, featuring an additional peninsula or countertop attached to one of the walls. This design provides even more storage and workspace, ideal for large families or avid cooks.

KITCHEN WITH WALK-IN PANTRY

Some kitchens feature a walk-in pantry adjacent to the main cooking area. This layout provides ample storage space for dry goods, canned items, and kitchen equipment.

Kitchens are one of the most essential and versatile spaces in a home, and come in various styles to suit different preferences and design aesthetics.

Each kitchen style offers a different ambiance and caters to diverse tastes and lifestyles. When designing or renovating a kitchen, considering these various styles can help you create a space that truly reflects your preferences and meets your functional needs. Here are some popular kitchen styles, each with its distinct characteristics:

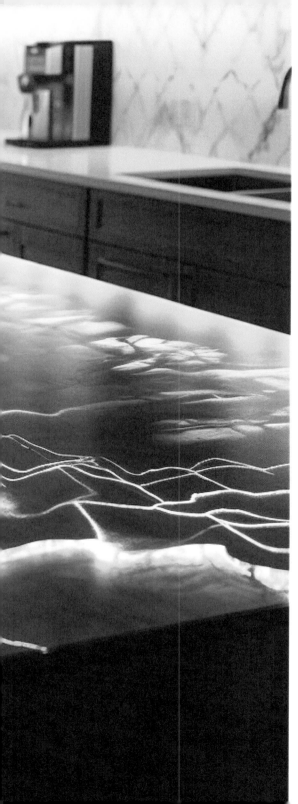

TRADITIONAL KITCHEN

The traditional kitchen exudes warmth and classic charm. It features rich, natural materials like wood for cabinetry, often with raised-panel doors. Details like crown molding and ornate hardware add a touch of elegance. Earthy colors and warm tones dominate the color palette, creating a cozy and inviting atmosphere.

MODERN KITCHEN

Sleek and minimalist, the modern kitchen embraces clean lines, smooth surfaces, and a clutter-free environment. Cabinets are often frameless with flat, glossy finishes or natural materials like metal or glass. The color palette leans towards neutral tones, and bold accents are used to add visual interest.

FARMHOUSE KITCHEN

Inspired by rustic and country aesthetics, the farmhouse kitchen showcases a mix of vintage and modern elements. It features open shelving, apron-front sinks, and distressed wood for cabinetry and furniture. Neutral colors, such as whites, creams, and pastels, create a charming and nostalgic ambiance.

INDUSTRIAL KITCHEN

Industrial kitchens draw inspiration from factories and warehouses, combining raw materials like metal, concrete, and exposed brick with utilitarian fixtures. Open shelves, stainless steel appliances, and minimal decor contribute to the raw and edgy look. Neutral colors with pops of metallic or bold accents complete the industrial vibe.

CONTEMPORARY KITCHEN

A blend of modern and traditional styles, the contemporary kitchen is characterized by its clean and streamlined design. It often features sleek cabinetry with simple hardware, and neutral colors are complemented by splashes of vibrant hues. Unique lighting fixtures and artful decor add personality to the space.

SCANDINAVIAN KITCHEN

Scandinavian kitchens are bright and airy, with a focus on functionality and simplicity. Light-colored wood and white cabinetry create a clean and fresh look, while natural light is maximized. Minimalist design, open shelving, and pops of color through textiles or decor reflect the Scandinavian lifestyle.

COTTAGE KITCHEN

The cottage kitchen exudes a cozy and quaint feel. It incorporates soft, pastel colors, floral patterns, and vintage-inspired accessories. Beadboard paneling, decorative molding, and decorative tile backsplashes contribute to the charming and cottage-like ambiance.

TRANSITIONAL KITCHEN

As a fusion of traditional and modern styles, the transitional kitchen offers a balanced and harmonious look. It features a mix of classic and contemporary elements, such as Shaker-style cabinets, simple hardware, and neutral colors with pops of vibrant accents.

MEDITERRANEAN KITCHEN

Inspired by the coastal regions of Southern Europe, the Mediterranean kitchen features warm and earthy colors, intricate tile work, and ornate details. Terra cotta tiles, wrought iron accents, and textured surfaces create a rustic and welcoming space.

ECLECTIC KITCHEN

An eclectic kitchen embraces a mix of styles, colors, and patterns. It is a highly personalized and creative space that reflects the homeowner's unique taste and personality. Elements from different styles are combined to create a visually stimulating and individualistic kitchen.

LECHIC BOHEMIAM FLAME

ECLECTIC PEARL TABLA

BATHROOM
DESIGN
101

Bathroom design styles encompass a wide range of aesthetics, from traditional and timeless to modern and minimalistic. Each style has its unique characteristics, materials, and fixtures that contribute to the overall ambiance of the space.

When choosing a bathroom design style, consider the architecture of your home, and the desired ambiance. Each style offers a unique character and can be tailored to suit your preferences and needs for a functional and aesthetically pleasing bathroom space.

TRADITIONAL BATHROOM

The traditional bathroom exudes elegance and charm with its classic design elements. It features ornate details, such as clawfoot tubs, pedestal sinks, and decorative molding. Rich, natural materials like marble, granite, and wood are often used for countertops and flooring. Colors tend to be soft and neutral, creating a serene and inviting atmosphere.

MODERN BATHROOM

The modern bathroom emphasizes clean lines and a minimalist approach. It features sleek fixtures, such as wall-mounted toilets and floating vanities, to create a streamlined look. Neutral colors and a simple color palette contribute to the contemporary feel. Modern bathrooms often incorporate the use of glass and chrome for a polished and airy appearance.

INDUSTRIAL BATHROOM

Inspired by the raw and rugged look of industrial spaces, the industrial bathroom features exposed brick walls, concrete floors, and metal fixtures. It embraces a utilitarian aesthetic with open shelving, exposed plumbing, and vintage lighting. Neutral colors and bold accents contribute to the edgy and urban vibe.

COASTAL BATHROOM

The coastal or beach-inspired bathroom evokes a relaxed and breezy atmosphere. It incorporates light colors like white, blue, and sandy beige, reminiscent of the ocean and the shore. Natural materials like wicker, seagrass, and driftwood add to the coastal charm. Nautical elements, such as rope accents and seashell decor, enhance the theme.

SCANDINAVIAN BATHROOM

The Scandinavian bathroom embraces simplicity and functionality. It features light colors, predominantly white, with touches of natural wood for warmth. Scandinavian bathrooms often have large windows to maximize natural light and create an airy ambiance. The design prioritizes functionality with minimal clutter.

FARMHOUSE BATHROOM

Inspired by rustic and country aesthetics, the farmhouse bathroom features a blend of vintage and modern elements. It incorporates shiplap walls, farmhouse sinks, and freestanding bathtubs. Neutral colors, such as whites and pastels, create a welcoming and charming space.

ART DECO BATHROOM

The Art Deco bathroom exudes glamour and luxury with its geometric patterns, bold colors, and luxurious materials. It features mirrored surfaces, black and white tiles, and gilded accents. Art Deco bathrooms often showcase dramatic lighting fixtures and elegant art deco-inspired accessories.

ECLECTIC BATHROOM

The eclectic bathroom is a mix of various styles and periods. It embraces an individualistic and creative approach, incorporating diverse materials, colors, and patterns. This style allows for personal expression and unique combinations that reflect the homeowner's personality.

TRANSITIONAL BATHROOM

As a blend of traditional and contemporary styles, the transitional bathroom strikes a balance between classic and modern elements. It features simple lines, neutral colors, and a mix of traditional and contemporary fixtures. This versatile style appeals to those seeking a timeless yet updated look.

JAPANESE ZEN BATHROOM

The Japanese Zen bathroom embodies tranquility and simplicity. It features natural materials like wood and stone, as well as elements of nature, such as indoor plants or bamboo accents. Neutral colors and clean lines create a serene and calming atmosphere, perfect for relaxation and rejuvenation.

MASTERFUL DESIGN: WHERE QUALITY MEETS INGENUITY.

In the world of high-end interior design and architecture, innovation is the driving force that continually reshapes the boundaries of possibility. This chapter explores the dynamic landscape where creativity and construction merge to create breathtaking spaces that redefine luxury.

THE FUSION OF ART AND ENGINEERING

At the pinnacle of high-end design and construction, artistry and engineering converge. Architects and designers embrace innovation as they envision spaces that not only meet functional needs but also captivate the senses. These professionals push beyond conventional aesthetics, striving to create environments that are both technically advanced and artistically inspiring.

MATERIALS OF THE FUTURE

Innovative design often starts with the selection of materials. Today's high-end projects are experimenting with materials that were once deemed unconventional. From the sleek fusion of glass and steel to the use of reclaimed wood and sustainable composites, designers are pushing the envelope, redefining what it means to create luxurious yet eco-conscious spaces.

TECHNOLOGY REDEFINED

The integration of technology into design and construction has revolutionized the industry. Smart homes have become smarter, with automation systems that seamlessly control lighting, climate, security, and more. Virtual reality and augmented reality have opened new dimensions in design, allowing clients to immerse themselves in their spaces before a single brick is laid.

SUSTAINABILITY AS A GUIDING PRINCIPLE

Innovation is also deeply intertwined with sustainability. Forward-thinking designers prioritize eco-friendly practices, from energy-efficient HVAC systems to solar panels and green roofs. Sustainable design not only reduces the environmental footprint but also enriches the quality of life within these spaces.

COLLABORATION AND VISION

Innovative projects thrive on collaboration. Architects, interior designers, engineers, and builders come together, each contributing their expertise to achieve a shared vision. This collaborative spirit fosters the cross-pollination of ideas, resulting in designs that are more than the sum of their parts.

A NEW AESTHETIC PARADIGM

Ultimately, innovative design and construction redefine the very notion of luxury. It's no longer solely about opulence and extravagance but about the seamless integration of technology, sustainability, and artistry. The end result is a harmonious marriage of form and function, where every detail contributes to an unparalleled living experience.

In this ever-evolving world of high-end interior design and architecture, innovation reigns supreme. It's the force that propels the industry forward, constantly challenging designers and builders to push beyond the limits of what's possible. The project showcased in this chapter by Three Eight Building Group, based in The Mornington Peninsula in Australia, serves as a testament to the incredible fusion of creativity and construction, illustrating the remarkable potential of innovative design.

The construction firm, **Three Eight Building Group**, behind this remarkable project has harnessed every millimeter of ingenious design and smart techniques, resulting in a space that seamlessly combines form and function. From the ground up, the emphasis on maximizing storage solutions has been meticulous, ensuring that every square millimeter is purposefully utilized. The commitment to high-end quality in both construction and finishes is evident in every detail, where precision and craftsmanship converge. This achievement stands as a testament to the relentless pursuit of excellence, where architectural innovation and unwavering dedication have culminated in a space that epitomizes the pinnacle of modern living. You can see more of their work by visiting **www.three8build.com.au**

HOW TO USE NATURAL STONES

IN THE SPACE AND HOW THEY BENEFIT US

Natural stones have long been cherished for their remarkable beauty, timeless elegance, and versatility in interior design. From the translucent allure of onyx to the enduring strength of granite, these stones have the power to transform any space into a visual masterpiece. This chapter delves into the captivating world of natural stones, showcasing their unique characteristics, and exploring the myriad ways they can enhance the aesthetics and functionality of interior spaces.

ONYX

Onyx is a mesmerizing gemstone with translucent layers that allow light to pass through, creating a captivating effect. Its delicate beauty and unique color variations make it a stunning choice for interior design. Onyx is often used to create backlit bar tops, kitchen countertops, accent walls, and decorative objects, adding an ethereal and enchanting touch to any space.

Onyx is believed to support inner strength and emotional healing. It is often used for grounding and balancing energy, helping individuals overcome negative emotions and build resilience.

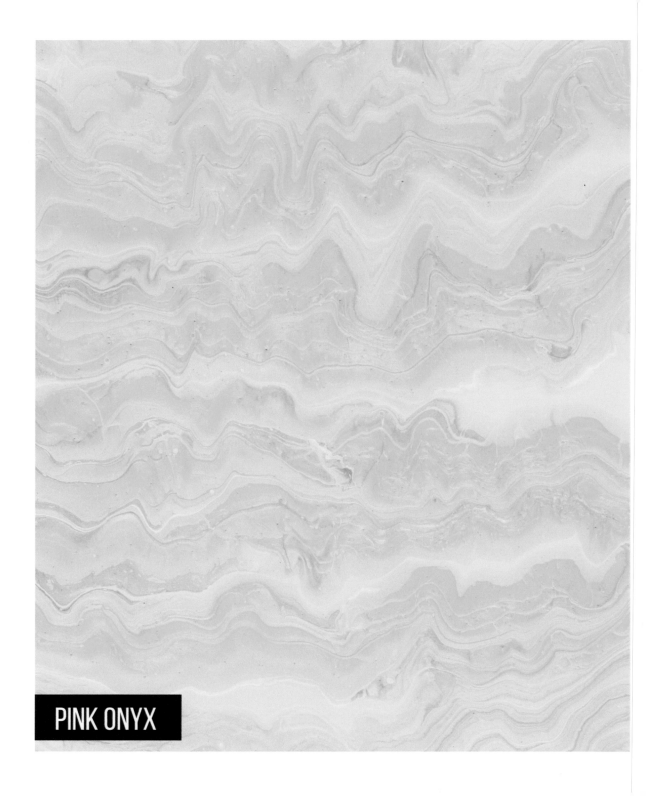

PINK ONYX

MARBLE DINING TABLE

MARBLE

Marble is a timeless and elegant natural stone known for its luxurious appearance. With its unique veining patterns and a wide array of colors, marble adds a touch of sophistication to interior design. It is commonly used for kitchen countertops, bathroom vanities, flooring, fireplace surrounds, and wall cladding, enhancing the aesthetic appeal and creating a sense of luxury and refinement.

Marble is known for its ability to promote clarity of mind, emotional balance, and spiritual grounding. It is considered a calming stone that helps soothe emotional stress, anxiety, and promotes a sense of tranquility.

GRANITE TABLE TOP

GRANITE

Granite is a durable and versatile igneous rock that combines strength with natural beauty. Available in various colors and patterns, granite is a popular choice for interior design. It is frequently used for kitchen countertops, backsplashes, tabletops, flooring, and staircases. Its resistance to heat, scratches, and stains, coupled with its timeless appeal, makes it a practical and enduring option for high-traffic areas.

Granite, prized for grounding energies and enhancing stability and strength, offers security, balance, and grounding in both physical and emotional aspects, while providing protection against negative energy.

LIMESTONE WALL

LIMESTONE

Limestone is a warm and inviting sedimentary rock that exudes a sense of natural beauty. Its earthy tones and textures create a cozy ambiance in interior spaces. Limestone finds its application in flooring, fireplace surrounds, accent walls, bathroom countertops, and exterior cladding. While it may require periodic sealing, limestone's durability and ability to withstand heavy foot traffic make it an attractive choice for both residential and commercial spaces.

Limestone is thought to encourage tranquility, soothing energy, and emotional stability. It is known for its calming properties, helping to alleviate stress and bring a sense of peace and serenity. Limestone is often used to create a harmonious atmosphere that promotes relaxation and a positive emotional state.

LE CHIC. DETALLE BOHEMIAM FLAME C

LE CHIC DETALLE ECLECTIC PEARL A

TRAVERTINE

Travertine is a distinct form of limestone known for its porous texture and unique voids, creating a visually appealing pattern. It adds an element of earthy elegance to interior design. Travertine is commonly used for flooring, wall cladding, bathroom countertops, shower enclosures, and outdoor paving. Its warm hues and natural variations make it an excellent choice for those seeking a rustic yet sophisticated look.

Travertine, a stone of harmony, balance, and connection to nature, inspires individuals to deepen their relationship with the environment, creating a serene and grounded atmosphere that fosters peace and well-being.

TREVI FOUNTAIN

QUARTZITE COUNTERTOP

QUARTZITE

Quartzite is a natural stone that offers the beauty of marble combined with the durability of granite. It features striking veining patterns and a wide palette of colors. Quartzite is highly versatile and finds its application in kitchen countertops, backsplashes, wall cladding, flooring, and stair treads. Its resistance to heat, scratches, and stains, along with its low maintenance requirements, make it an ideal choice for both residential and commercial spaces.

Quartzite, renowned for its ability to amplify spiritual growth, clarity, and positive energy flow, enhances intuition and spiritual awareness, creating a high-vibration environment for personal growth and deep insights.

SANDSTONE

Sandstone is a versatile natural stone that showcases a diverse array of colors and textures. Its warm and earthy tones, combined with its naturRal variations, add a sense of natural beauty to interior spaces. Sandstone finds its application in flooring, wall cladding, pavers, pool surrounds, and garden sculptures. Its ability to withstand extreme weather conditions makes it suitable for both indoor and outdoor use, offering a seamless connection between spaces.

Sandstone is known for promoting creativity, strength, and emotional well-being. This stone is associated with nurturing energies that stimulate imagination and creative expression. Sandstone is often used to create an uplifting and inspiring environment that encourages self-expression and emotional healing.

ANTELOPE CANYON SANDSTONES

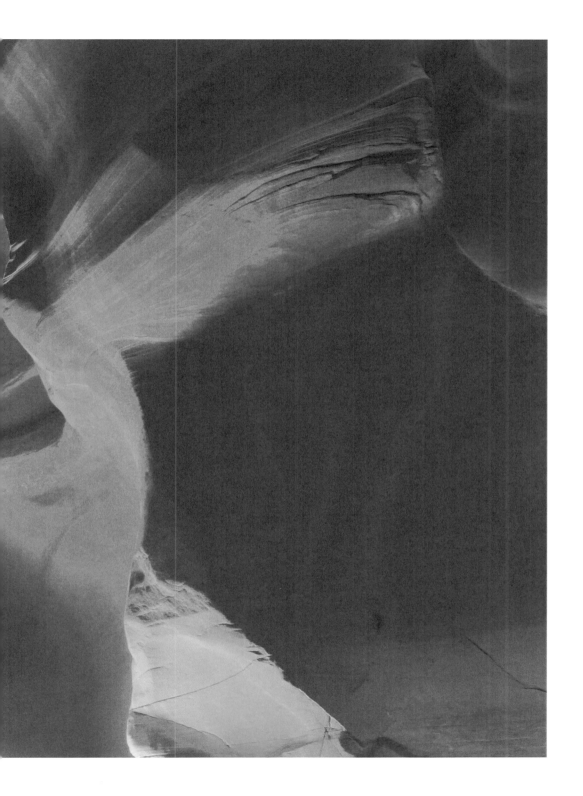

SLATE ROOFING

SLATE

Slate is a fine-grained metamorphic rock known for its distinctive texture and rich, earthy tones. It offers a unique blend of ruggedness and sophistication. Slate is commonly used for flooring, wall cladding, roofing, fireplace hearths, and outdoor pathways. Its natural cleft surface and durable nature make it an excellent choice for both contemporary and traditional design styles.

Slate, facilitating grounding, protection, and resilience, stabilizes the energy field, fostering a grounded and centered state during challenging times, while creating a protective shield against negativity and nurturing inner strength.

92

QUARTZ

Quartz is an engineered stone composed of natural quartz crystals mixed with resin and pigments. It is a versatile material that offers a wide range of colors and patterns. Quartz is known for its sleek and modern appearance, making it a popular choice for contemporary interior design. It is commonly used for kitchen countertops, vanity tops, backsplashes, shower walls, and fireplace surrounds. With its durability, low maintenance, and resistance to stains and scratches, quartz provides a practical and elegant solution for various applications.

Quartz is believed to amplify energy, purify the mind, and balance emotions. This stone is considered a powerful healer and energy amplifier, enhancing positive energy flow and dispelling negative energies. Quartz is often used to cleanse and harmonize the energy field, promoting mental clarity, emotional balance, and overall well-being.

QUARTZ COUNTERTOP

SOAPSTONE BACKSPLASH AND COUNTER

SOAPSTONE

Soapstone is a soft and heat-resistant stone known for its smooth texture and rich, dark color variations. It exudes a sense of understated elegance and warmth. Soapstone is often used for kitchen countertops, sink basins, fireplace hearths, bathroom vanity tops, and carving and sculpting. Its natural resistance to heat and stains, along with its unique aging process that develops a rich patina over time, makes it a preferred choice for those seeking a distinct and durable surface.

Soapstone is thought to encourage calmness, emotional healing, and nurturing energy. This stone is associated with tranquility and emotional stability, providing a sense of comfort and support during times of stress or emotional upheaval. Soapstone is often used to create a soothing and nurturing atmosphere that promotes emotional healing and self-care.

BASALT

Basalt is a volcanic rock characterized by its fine-grained texture and durability. It is known for its dark coloration and strength. Basalt is commonly used for flooring, wall cladding, countertops, pavers, and exterior facades. Its versatility and ability to withstand heavy use and extreme weather conditions make it a suitable choice for both interior and exterior applications.

Basalt, renowned for enhancing strength, stability, and connection to Earth's energy, releases blocked energies for physical and emotional healing, creating a harmonious environment that fosters personal growth, transformation, and energetic alignment.

BASALT FLOOR

SERPENTINE STONE

SERPENTINE

Serpentine is a unique stone known for its smooth and waxy texture, with various shades of green running through it. It offers a distinct aesthetic appeal. Serpentine finds its application in flooring, wall cladding, tabletops, decorative objects, and fireplace surrounds. Its natural beauty and vibrant color variations create a captivating visual impact in interior spaces.

Stimulates healing, transformation, and energy flow. Creates harmony, supports growth and alignment.

GNEISS STONE

GNEISS

Gneiss is a durable metamorphic rock known for its distinctive banding and granular texture. It offers a balance of strength and aesthetic appeal. Gneiss finds its application in flooring, wall cladding, staircases, countertops, and exterior paving. Its versatile nature, combined with its unique patterns and colors, allows for creative and striking design possibilities.

Inspires balance, stability, inner strength. Grounding energies foster resilience. Creates harmony, supports equilibrium.

SCHIST

Schist is a metamorphic rock with a coarse-grained texture and layered appearance, giving it a unique visual appeal. It is characterized by its rustic charm and natural beauty. Schist is commonly used for flooring, wall cladding, countertops, landscaping features, and water features. Its durability, coupled with its rich colors and textures, make it a popular choice for creating a distinctive and rugged ambiance.

Schist is thought to promote adaptability, grounding, and harmonious energy flow. This stone is associated with flexibility and the ability to adapt to changing circumstances. Schist is often used to create a sense of stability and balance, allowing individuals to navigate life's challenges with grace and resilience.

SCHIST FIREPLACE

THE FOUNDATIONS OF SUSTAINABILITY: DESIGNING TOMORROW WITH INNOVATIVE AND SUSTAINABLE SURFACES

In the realm of design and construction, sustainability has risen to prominence as a guiding principle that not only shapes the aesthetics of our built environment but also defines the legacy we leave for future generations. As we confront the looming challenges of climate change and environmental degradation on a global scale, our choices as architects, builders, and designers have never held more significance. In this chapter, we delve into the world of global sustainability in design and construction, with a particular focus on the manifold benefits of using high-value innovative and sustainable surfaces.

DEKTON

THE GLOBAL IMPERATIVE

Sustainability is no longer a choice but a global imperative. Our planet's finite resources are stretched to their limits, and the environmental consequences of past practices have become undeniable. It is in this context that sustainability emerges as a moral and practical obligation, guiding the way we shape our world. Design and construction, which contribute significantly to resource consumption and greenhouse gas emissions, are at the forefront of this transformation.

THE SUSTAINABLE SURFACE REVOLUTION

Amidst this transformation, high-value innovative and sustainable surfaces have emerged as beacons of hope and promise. These surfaces, a testament to human ingenuity and ecological responsibility, offer a compelling blend of contemporary elegance and a commitment to preserving the environment. What sets them apart is not just their aesthetic appeal but also their journey from concept to construction site.

ECO-FRIENDLY PRODUCTION

High-value innovative and sustainable surfaces begin their journey with eco-friendly production practices. Manufacturers like Cosentino, a global leader in sustainable surface solutions, are reimagining their processes to minimize environmental impacts. They employ advanced technology to reduce energy consumption and waste generation, ensuring that these surfaces are created with sustainability at their core.

LE CHIC VERSAILLES IVORY

VICTORIAN SILVER TABLA

COSENTINO: LEADING THE WAY

For someone as particular as myself, who aligns only with the most trusted and reputable partners in the industry and carefully selects materials for projects, mentioning Cosentino in this book is a testament to years of trust and unwavering commitment to sustainability. Cosentino stands as an exemplar of a company at the forefront of sustainability in the world of innovative and low silica surfaces. They have earned my trust through their consistent dedication to responsible sourcing, energy efficiency, waste reduction, and the creation of surfaces that endure.

RESPONSIBLE SOURCING

Cosentino sources materials responsibly, selecting natural stone and recycled materials with a focus on minimizing the environmental impact of quarrying and extraction. For someone meticulous about materials, knowing that Cosentino prioritizes responsible sourcing aligns perfectly with my ethos.

ENERGY EFFICIENCY

In their manufacturing processes, Cosentino has invested in state-of-the-art technology to reduce energy consumption and emissions. As someone who values efficiency, their commitment to energy efficiency not only reduces their operational impact but also results in surfaces with lower embodied energy.

WASTE REDUCTION

My attention to detail extends to waste reduction, and Cosentino is dedicated to minimizing waste throughout their production processes. Their recycling initiatives and efficient material usage ensure that minimal waste ends up in landfills.

LONG-LASTING IMPACT

My projects are not just about creating spaces; they are about leaving a legacy. Cosentino's surfaces are designed with longevity in mind. Their durability and resilience ensure that structures adorned with Cosentino materials stand the test of time, reducing the need for frequent replacements and conserving resources while minimizing waste generation.

LOCAL SOURCING AND COMMUNITY IMPACT

Like many sustainable surface manufacturers, Cosentino recognizes the importance of local sourcing in reducing transportation-related emissions. They often partner with local communities, providing jobs and economic opportunities in regions that need them most. For someone who values community impact, this aspect of sustainability fosters a sense of global community invested in a sustainable future.

AESTHETIC AND FUNCTIONAL EXCELLENCE

Cosentino's innovative surfaces offer more than just ecological benefits; they elevate the aesthetic and functional aspects of design. These surfaces are engineered with creativity and functionality in mind, transforming spaces with their unique textures, colors, and patterns while contributing to energy efficiency.

In the quest for global sustainability in design and construction, companies like Cosentino play a pivotal role. Their dedication to responsible sourcing, energy efficiency, waste reduction, and long-lasting impact sets a high standard for the industry. For someone particular about alignment and trust, mentioning Cosentino in this book signifies the culmination of years of partnership with a company that shares the unwavering commitment to a sustainable future. The journey begins with companies like Cosentino, and their ripple effects extend across continents, shaping a world that we can be proud to pass on to generations yet to come.

LECHIC TABLA ROMANTIC ASH

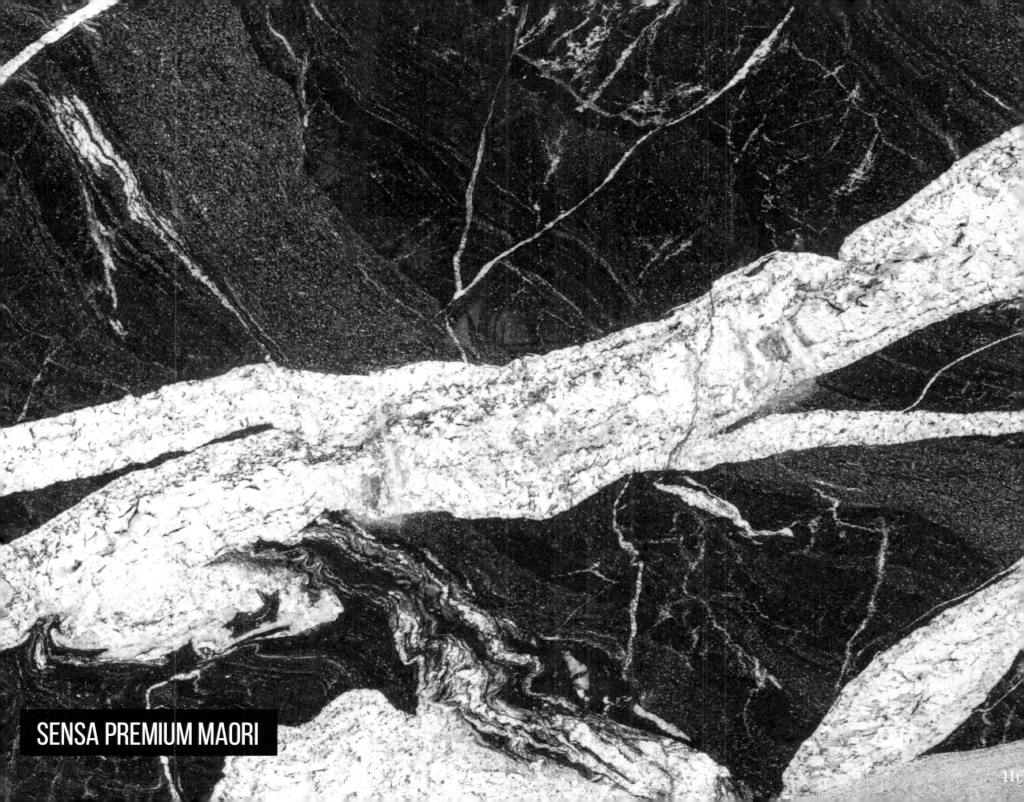

SENSA PREMIUM MAORI

FROM NOW TO WOW

Interior design is an exhilarating realm where ideas flourish and overwhelm us, whether we're envisioning grand spaces or cozy corners. As we dive into the depths of creativity, a fundamental question echoes in our minds: "Where do I begin?"

Look at it for a minute like dress sense; when I do master classes, I have a segment where I come out dressed in one color (monochromatic). Then, I start adding things to reveal the many different looks I can make using the same base color. Even if the color were to stay the same, it's the details and how it's worn that makes the difference; you get a variety of totally different looks.

Here's my point, The properties are the same, whether you're dressing up or styling property. Interior design is like designing an outfit on a bigger scale!

As an interior designer, it's important to work with the existing elements that cannot be changed, such as plumbing, existing furniture, load-bearing walls, breathtaking views, or cherished artworks. From there, build your design scheme around these key elements.

If you have a blank canvas, begin with the most significant or costly area, often starting from the flooring and working your way up. This approach allows you to weave your creative magic and bring the space to life.

STONIKA XGLOSS COLLECTION HELENA

VERSAILLES IVORY TABLA

120

MAJLIS ROOM
THE DECADENT SPACE

THE GRAND ENTRANCE

I have an inherent passion for embracing the utilization of exceptionally spacious entrance doors while meticulously upholding the principles of proportion, balance, and aesthetic cohesion. In my earnest belief, the magnitude of the entrance doors directly corresponds to the enormity of the warm embrace and heartfelt reception that a home can offer. Hence, it becomes an utmost priority to accord the entrance the reverence it deserves, as it holds the power to leave an indelible impression.

When evaluating an entrance, several crucial factors must be considered. Does it create an inviting and sophisticated atmosphere that aligns with your client's aspirations? Does it reflect their desired aesthetic, exuding elegance and class? Additionally, should the entrance blend seamlessly with the neighborhood's architectural fabric or make a bold statement of its own? Furthermore, it is vital to ensure a smooth transition between indoor and outdoor spaces, fostering a harmonious interplay.

To enhance the entrance, consider exploring options that can elevate its allure. A simple change in color palette can infuse vibrancy, while carefully selected statement pieces can add character and captivate attention. By actively presenting these alternatives to clients, you demonstrate your commitment to their satisfaction and surpassing expectations. This approach ensures the creation of an entrance that truly embodies their unique vision.

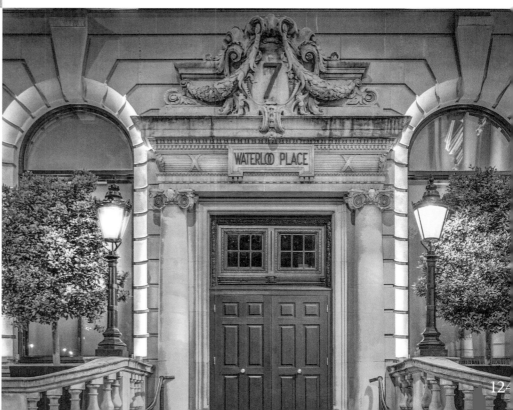

GLAM, BAM, THANK YOU MA'AM

The glamorous image often associated with interior designers reclining on fine furniture with a glass of champagne can be misleading. In reality, interior design involves creative problem–solving and a significant amount of paperwork, comprising about 20 to 30 percent of the work. Despite the seemingly endless tasks, the profession is highly rewarding. Witnessing a grand vision come to life brings immense joy to both the client and the designer.

However, it is crucial to prioritize purpose over mere aesthetics. Successful design should be based on understanding its potential for success, rather than relying solely on visual appeal. While the lifestyle of an interior designer may have elements of luxury, it typically accounts for only 10 to 20 percent of their time. Nevertheless, some designers, like myself, have been fortunate enough to make luxury a significant part of their career, enjoying it 90 percent of the time.

GET FABULOUS WITH WALL ART

Wanting to change things up and add life to your living space, look into high quality wall decals. These vinyl wall stickers are easy to position, remove and reposition and come in different shapes and sizes. Try baroque motifs, modern contemporary, retro funk, minimalist geometrics or kids' motifs—all of them are just fabulous.

Textural papers designs can be extraordinary. They use substances such as scratched metals and tarnished finishes in bronze and charcoal. New textile technology is bringing together fashion and interior design and furnishings. Innovation with materials include mixing the primitive/archaic with the futuristic/modern essentially bridging the gap between modern technology and traditional techniques in non-traditional compositions.

Here are a few textural paper designs to keep in mind: New non-woven techno fabrics offer iridescence, luminosity and luster with feather-light microfiber sheers used in multi-layers and as veiling; rubberized and plasticized effects; paper like effects; cob-web like netting; pearlised, crinkled, irregular weaves; dense felts and thick cord velvets. Patterns include leaves, embroideries, multi-stripes, spots, circles and squares.

128

16 STEPS TO PUT SPUNK INTO YOUR SPACE

1. Incorporate sound and movement into interiors, such as choosing fabric that rustles in the breeze or using suspended screens on aluminum rods.

2. Consider adding luxury touches to everyday items. For instance, special glassware for water, a meticulously made bed, or the inviting scent of a candle.

3. Reduce clutter by minimizing personal belongings and focusing on essential items.

4. Highlight objects that hold personal significance.

5. When opting for a more modern design, prioritize comfort and functionality.

6. Take the opportunity to combine warm and traditional with minimalist.

7. New layout concepts for apartments and homes with an emphasis on multi-purpose rooms, flexibility and moveable walls.

8. Showcase beautifully crafted pieces and emphasize their uniqueness.

9. Update antiques to bring a new approach to romanticism and modern, like using chandeliers.

10. Play around with the scale of patterns or combining elements of technology in fabrics.

11. Mix of techno with traditional (or natural) in textiles to give them modernity.

12. Crystal is making a comeback. Try to cut, etch, sandblast, use crystal drops or color them.

13. Have you tried velvet?

14. Are you aiming for indulgence?

15. Do aspire for more glamour?

16. Drama comes with exceptional lighting. Mix the contemporary and traditional.

TABLEWEAR

Here are some simple ideas to get you into the Groove of styling with tableware, whether it be your own or for clients.

1. Incorporate the elegance of antique silver into your design.

2. Consider the allure of cut crystal, whether etched, frosted, or in vibrant colors.

3. Explore the use of opaque glass or solid-shaped glasses for a distinctive touch.

4. Embrace the enchantment of candlelight to infuse your space with glamour and romance.

5. Enhance the charm of your design with unique furniture pieces that exude old-world appeal.

6. Utilize table decorations to create an ambient atmosphere within the room.

FINISHES

Here are some ideas to get you into the thinking of millions of possibilities of finishes

1. Experiment with burnished surfaces or exceptionally shiny finishes to add a touch of sophistication.

2. Explore the captivating effect of iridescence or colors that shift when viewed from different angles.

3. Have you contemplated the allure of mirrored walls?

4. Get creative with transparency, crystal elements, white glass, or lustrous materials to introduce intriguing visual elements.

5. Consider the velvety elegance of matte paint finishes or explore the depth of texture they can provide.

There are fabulous wallpapers available including Swarovski wallpapers which really do have Swarovski crystals in them. (See images)

ARCHISCULPT STUDIO'S LEADERSHIP IN 3D ARCHITECTURAL VISUALIZATION

In the dynamic realm of design and innovation, 3D Architectural Visualization stands as a revolutionary force, reshaping our perception and interaction with the world. Beyond the constraints of traditional 2D representations, this transformative technology serves as a powerful communication tool. At the forefront of this visual revolution is ArchiSculpt Studio, a pioneering leader in the field of 3D Architectural Visualization.

The essence of 3D Architectural Visualization lies in its remarkable ability to bridge the gap between imagination and reality. Architects, designers, and creatives in diverse industries leverage its potential to bring concepts and ideas to life. Whether it's architectural design, product development, urban planning, or the specific requirements of property and real estate professionals and developers, 3D Architectural Visualization has become an indispensable tool, propelling innovation to new heights. A primary advantage of 3D Architectural Visualization is its capacity to offer a realistic and immersive experience. ArchiSculpt Studio, with its advanced techniques and skilled artisans, meticulously crafts virtual worlds that mirror reality with astonishing accuracy. This immersive quality proves invaluable in architectural design, allowing stakeholders to explore spaces before construction commences. Clients can embark on virtual tours through buildings, visualizing every detail, from room layouts to the interplay of light and shadow.

3D Architectural Visualization plays a pivotal role in marketing and presentation, catering specifically to the needs of property and real estate professionals and developers. ArchiSculpt Studio's expertise extends to creating compelling visualizations that surpass static images. Dynamic animations and interactive presentations breathe life into projects, enabling stakeholders to engage with designs in unprecedented ways. This not only enhances communication between designers and clients but also serves as a potent marketing tool, captivating audiences and conveying the vision behind each project.

The efficiency and precision offered by 3D Architectural Visualization are invaluable in product design, development, and, crucially, in meeting the requirements of property and real estate professionals. ArchiSculpt Studio, with its meticulous attention to detail, expedites the process, bringing the built environment to market faster and with greater precision.

In the realm of urban planning, 3D Architectural Visualization becomes a powerful tool for envisioning the future—a future equally relevant for property and real estate professionals and developers. ArchiSculpt Studio contributes to the creation of smart cities by visualizing how infrastructure, public spaces, and architectural elements converge to shape cohesive urban environments. City planners, real estate professionals, and developers can make informed decisions, considering the visual impact and functionality of their choices before implementation.

3D Architectural Visualization, led by innovators like ArchiSculpt Studio, has become indispensable in modern design. Its ability to transcend the limitations of traditional representation methods redefines how concepts are perceived, created, and communicated. As technology advances, the impact of 3D Architectural Visualization is set to grow, ushering in a future where the boundaries between imagination and reality seamlessly blur. ArchiSculpt Studio, with its visionary approach, remains at the forefront of this visual revolution, pushing the boundaries of what is possible in the world of 3D Architectural Visualization to meet the diverse needs of professionals across various industries, including property and real estate.

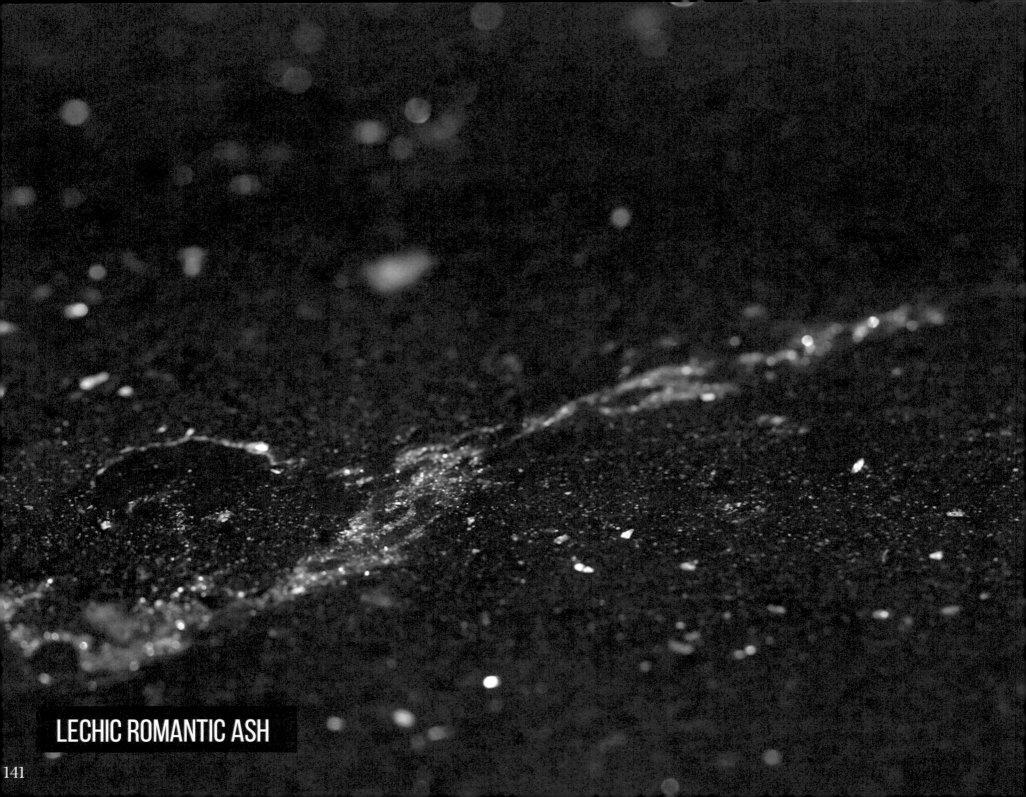

LECHIC ROMANTIC ASH

141

PARISIAN BLEU TABLA

MIRRORS

HERE ARE SOME IDEAS OF HOW TO USE MIRRORS IN INTERIOR DESIGN

DECORATIVE WINDOWS

Just like windows, mirrors add light and depth to the room interior, so feel free to use them as decorative windows that could be installed in any place you wish. Keep in mind that mirrors have a unique ability both to reflect and accentuate hues and views from neighboring walls and thus create striking effect.

FOCAL POINT

Mirror can become a perfect focal point of any room. It shouldn't necessarily be a big wall mirror; even a small mirror in bold framing can become a center of attention.

ENLARGING SPACES

We designers tend to use mirrors in small rooms since they are able to visually expand it. Just make sure it reflects nice views. Mirrors cannot only enlarge space, but also brighten it up and become an additional source of lighting.

By strategically placing mirrors opposite windows or light sources, natural light can bounce off their surfaces, creating a sense of openness and illumination.

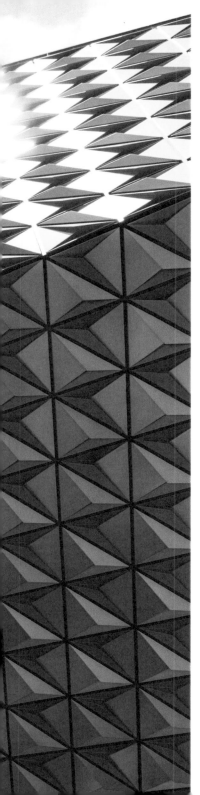

STATEMENT OBJECT

Large floor mirrors allow making a statement in a narrow room and bring a dramatic effect, which cannot be accomplished by other décor elements.

MIRRORS AS ART OBJECTS

You will be surprised to find out that mirrors can serve as full-fledged art objects. Simply play with them and try to hang a group of mirrors on a certain wall. Ensure the mirrors are proportional to each other and to the wall: don't try to hang a multitude of small mirrors on a big wall.

DÉCOR ELEMENT

Besides carrying a reflective function, mirrors make up perfect décor elements. A large mirror in a striking frame can instantly boost an interior of your room.

ENTRYWAY

Mirrors are versatile objects that find their place in entryways, dining rooms, and areas lacking natural light. They create a distinct ambiance when paired with candles, art objects, and unique lighting.

Creating larger and decadent interior spaces with mirrors can be a wonderful way to transform any space. Mirrors have the unique ability to reflect light, add depth, and create the illusion of more space. By strategically placing mirrors and employing some interior design techniques, you can achieve stunning results. Here's a guide to help you achieve this.

CHOOSE THE RIGHT LOCATION

First and foremost, identify the areas where you want to create the illusion of more space. Mirrors work best in rooms with natural light sources and should be placed opposite windows or doors to reflect the outside view and bring in more light.

SELECT THE APPROPRIATE SIZE AND SHAPE

The size and shape of the mirrors are essential in achieving your desired effect. Larger mirrors can make a room feel more spacious, while tall mirrors can add a sense of height to a space. Additionally, consider the shape of the mirror – round and oval mirrors can soften the overall look, while rectangular and square mirrors provide a more structured feel.

USE MIRRORS AS FOCAL POINTS

To create an elegant and eye-catching interior, use mirrors as focal points in your design. Choose mirrors with decorative frames that complement the style of the room and draw attention to their beauty.

MIRROR WALL

One of the most effective ways to open up a space is by creating a mirror wall. This involves covering an entire wall with mirrors or placing multiple mirrors together to create a continuous reflective surface. Be cautious not to overdo it, as too many mirrors can become overwhelming.

MIRRORED FURNITURE AND ACCESSORIES

Incorporate mirrored furniture pieces like cabinets, coffee tables, or side tables into your design. They not only serve functional purposes but also add elegance and reflect light throughout the room. Use mirrored accessories like vases, trays, or picture frames to further enhance the overall effect.

MIRROR PLACEMENT TO REFLECT LIGHT

Position mirrors to reflect both natural and artificial light sources. This not only brightens up the room but also creates a sense of openness. Placing mirrors near or opposite light fixtures can bounce light around the space, making it appear more spacious.

STRATEGIC PLACEMENT FOR VIEWS

To create the illusion of additional space, position mirrors to reflect appealing views or architectural elements. For example, you can place a mirror to reflect a beautiful piece of artwork or a stunning outdoor landscape.

CONSIDER MIRRORED DOORS AND PANELS

Mirrored doors for closets or cabinets can make a room feel larger and serve a practical purpose at the same time. You can also use mirrored panels on wardrobe doors or even as wall cladding to create an opulent and spacious ambiance.

GROUPING MIRRORS

Create an impactful visual display by grouping mirrors of different sizes and shapes together. You can arrange them in a gallery-style layout on a wall or even use mirrored tiles to create interesting patterns.

KEEP IT CLEAN AND CLUTTER-FREE

Regularly clean the mirrors to maintain their reflective quality. Additionally, ensure that the mirrors and their surroundings are clutter-free to allow the space to feel open and elegant.

In conclusion, mirrors can be powerful tools in interior design, transforming small and dull spaces into larger, brighter, and more elegant environments. By carefully selecting the right size, shape, and placement of mirrors, you can create a beautiful and functional interior that leaves a lasting impression on anyone who enters the room.

BLACK AND WHITE PHOTOGRAPHY

ELEGANT SIMPLICITY

Black and white photography strips away the distractions of color, allowing viewers to focus on the essence of the image. The simplicity of black and white images creates a sense of elegance and sophistication, making them a perfect fit for various interior design styles, from modern and minimalist to classic and traditional.

TIMELESS APPEAL

Unlike color photographs that may be subject to changing trends and palettes, black and white photography is timeless. These images evoke a sense of nostalgia, creating a connection between the past and the present. They can resonate with viewers of all ages and backgrounds, making them a versatile choice for any interior space.

HARMONIOUS INTEGRATION

Black and white photographs seamlessly blend into various color schemes and design elements. Whether it's a vibrant and colorful interior or a more subdued and monochromatic palette, black and white images can be effortlessly incorporated without clashing with other decorative elements.

VISUAL RESTFULNESS

Black and white photography can provide a sense of visual restfulness in an interior space. In environments where there's already an abundance of colors and patterns, monochromatic images can serve as a visual break, creating a harmonious and balanced atmosphere.

VERSATILITY IN ARTISTIC STYLES

Black and white photography encompasses a wide range of artistic styles, from landscape and architecture to portraiture and abstract art. This diversity allows you to curate a collection of photographs that align with the theme and ambiance of the interior space, reflecting the personality and interests of the occupants.

CONTRAST AND TEXTURE

In black and white photography, contrast plays a significant role in creating visually striking images. The interplay of light and shadows adds depth and dimension to the photographs, making them visually captivating. Additionally, black and white photography accentuates textures, making details more pronounced and adding tactile interest to the decor.

PERSONAL EXPRESSION

Photographs often capture meaningful moments, places, or people in our lives. By displaying black and white photographs in your interior space, you can infuse the area with personal stories and memories, adding an intimate and emotional touch to the decor.

FOCAL POINTS AND CONVERSATION STARTERS

Well-chosen black and white photographs can serve as focal points and conversation starters in a room. Whether it's a large framed print above a fireplace or a gallery wall of smaller images in a hallway, they draw attention and create a focal point around which the rest of the design can revolve.

THE FABULOUS WORLD OF FABRIC

Using decadent fabrics in interior spaces can elevate the overall ambiance, adding a touch of luxury, comfort, and sophistication. Decadent fabrics are often rich in texture, high-quality, and visually appealing, making them perfect for creating a lavish and indulgent atmosphere.

Fabulous fabrics in interior spaces can instantly transform a room into a luxurious and indulgent haven. Whether it's through upholstery, window treatments, bedding, rugs, or soft furnishings, incorporating rich and textured fabrics adds depth, comfort, and elegance to the overall design. The key is to balance these fabrics with complementary elements to create a harmonious and visually stunning interior. Here's how you too can incorporate decadent fabrics in any space.

LUXURIOUS UPHOLSTERY

Opt for decadent fabrics like velvet, silk, or satin for upholstered furniture pieces such as sofas, armchairs, and ottomans. These fabrics have a plush and sumptuous feel that instantly enhances the comfort and elegance of the space.

ELEGANT DRAPERIES

Use opulent fabrics for window treatments, such as floor-length curtains made of silk, brocade, or jacquard. These heavy, flowing fabrics not only provide privacy and light control but also create a sense of grandeur and drama in the room.

RICH BEDDING

Dress your beds in decadent fabrics like high-thread-count Egyptian cotton or silk. Layering the bed with luxurious duvets, throws, and decorative pillows adds depth and texture to the bedroom, creating a lavish retreat.

PLUSH RUGS AND CARPETS

Invest in thick and soft rugs or carpets made from materials like wool, cashmere, or mohair. Placing these decadent floor coverings in key areas, such as the living room or bedroom, provides a warm and inviting feel underfoot.

DESIGNER WALLPAPER

Consider using decadent fabric-inspired wallpaper to add depth and interest to the walls. Textured and embossed wallpapers with intricate patterns can create a luxurious backdrop for the entire interior.

DECORATIVE THROWS AND PILLOWS

Accessorize furniture with decorative throws and pillows made from rich fabrics like velvet, brocade, or faux fur. These plush accents add pops of color and texture, making the space feel inviting and cozy.

CUSTOMIZED SOFT FURNISHINGS

Opt for custom-made soft furnishings, such as cushions, tablecloths, and napkins, using decadent fabrics that complement the overall design theme. Customization allows you to tailor the fabric choices to suit your style and preferences perfectly.

ELEGANT CANOPIES AND VALANCES

In bedrooms or dining areas, consider using decadent fabrics to create canopies or valances over beds or windows. These elements add a sense of opulence and grandeur to the space.

STATEMENT WALL PANELS

Install wall panels covered in luxurious fabric to create a striking focal point in the room. Upholstered panels can add texture and visual interest to otherwise plain walls.

LUXURIOUS HEADBOARDS

For a lavish bedroom, choose an upholstered headboard in a decadent fabric. This creates a luxurious focal point and adds a sense of coziness and comfort to the room.

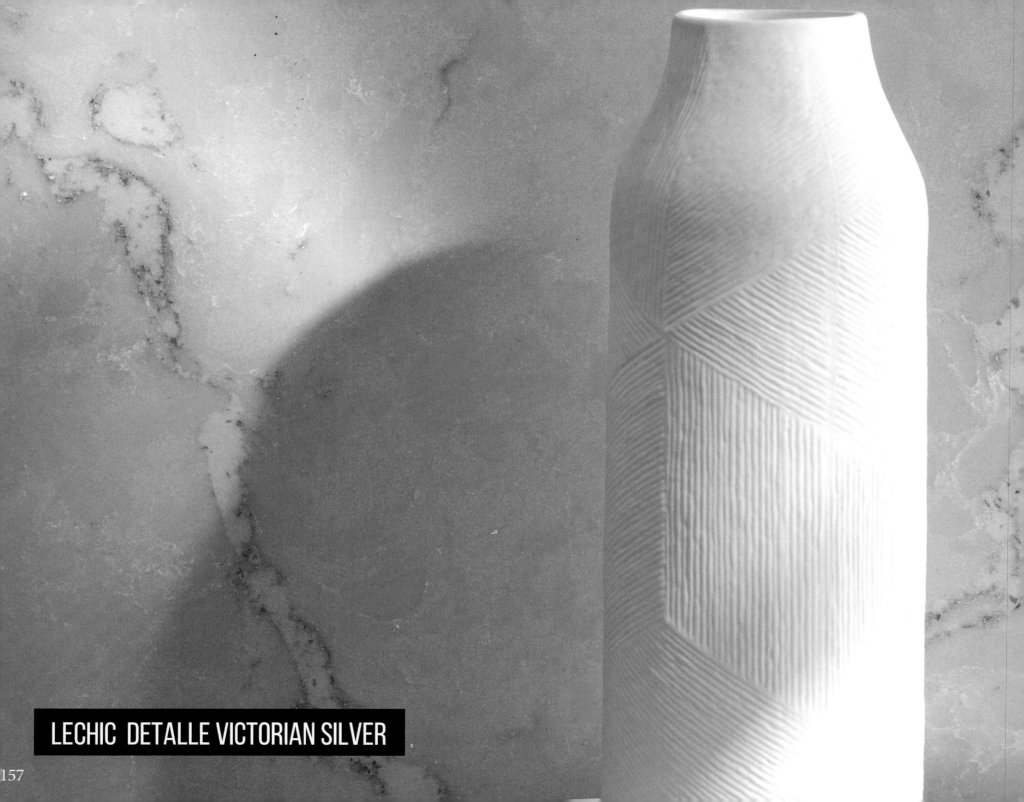

LECHIC DETALLE VICTORIAN SILVER

LECHIC DETALLE ECLECTIC PEARL B

COLORS AND PATTERNS

Selecting colors, patterns, materials, and textures for an interior design scheme involves thoughtful planning and consideration. By defining the purpose and style, creating a cohesive color palette, incorporating patterns and textures, and balancing the elements effectively, you can achieve a stunning and personalized interior that enhances the functionality and aesthetic appeal of the space.

Choosing the right colors, patterns, materials, and textures for an interior design scheme is a creative process that requires careful consideration and planning. Here's a step-by-step guide to help you make informed decisions and create a cohesive and visually pleasing interior.

DEFINE THE PURPOSE AND STYLE

Start by understanding the purpose of the space and the style you want to achieve. Consider factors like the function of the room, the mood you want to evoke, and the overall theme. This will serve as a foundation for your color and material choices.

CHOOSE A COLOR PALETTE

Select a color palette that aligns with your desired style and complements the space's purpose. Begin with a dominant color that sets the tone, then add two to three complementary or contrasting colors. Use color swatches and paint samples to visualize how the colors will interact in the space.

CONSIDER PATTERNS

Incorporate patterns sparingly to add visual interest. Mix patterns of different scales and styles to create depth. Stripes, geometric shapes, florals, and abstract patterns can all be used, but be mindful not to overuse patterns, as it can create visual clutter.

CREATE VISUAL BALANCE

Achieve visual balance by distributing colors, patterns, materials, and textures evenly throughout the space. Avoid placing too many bold elements in one area; instead, spread them out to create a harmonious flow.

TEST SAMPLES

Before committing to a particular color, pattern, material, or texture, obtain samples and test them in the actual space. Lighting conditions and the surrounding elements can influence how colors and materials appear, so it's crucial to evaluate them in context.

SELECT MATERIALS AND TEXTURES

Choose materials and textures that enhance the overall aesthetic and functionality of the space. Consider the tactile qualities of the materials – for example, soft fabrics for cozy areas and smooth surfaces for a sleek and modern look. Incorporate a variety of materials, such as wood, metal, glass, fabric, and stone, to add richness to the design.

CONSIDER THE MOOD AND EMOTION

Colors, patterns, materials, and textures can evoke different moods and emotions. For instance, warm colors like red and orange can create a cozy and inviting atmosphere, while cool colors like blue and green promote a sense of calmness and relaxation. Choose elements that align with the desired emotional impact.

CREATE A FOCAL POINT

Use colors, patterns, materials, or textures to establish a focal point in the room. This could be a vibrant accent wall, a patterned rug, a textured artwork, or an eye-catching piece of furniture. The focal point draws attention and adds character to the space.

CONSIDER PRACTICALITY

While aesthetics are essential, also consider the practicality of your choices. Choose materials and textures that are durable and easy to maintain, especially in high-traffic areas.

TRUST YOUR INSTINCTS

Ultimately, interior design is a creative expression of your preferences and personality. Trust your instincts and choose elements that resonate with you and create a space that reflects your unique style and taste.

LUSCIOUS LIGHTING

Knowing the basics of functional and decorative lighting is essential for creating a well-designed lighting scheme. There are three types of illumination to consider: general lighting, task lighting, and accent lighting, which, when combined, result in decorative lighting. Decorative lighting enhances the mood and meaning of a space, emphasizing shapes, textures, and room highlights. Variation in light levels and sources, such as chandeliers and pendants, can create focal points and indicate the purpose of different rooms. Consider the activities, locations, and timing of events when planning a lighting scheme, as different intensities may be required. Seeking assistance from trained personnel at lighting stores or home remodeling centers can help you make informed choices based on your floor plans and decorating preferences.

GENERAL LIGHTING

General lighting, also known as ambient lighting, ensures overall illumination and safety in a space. It provides even illumination throughout a room and can be achieved with different types of fixtures. Uplights, like torchiere lamps and wall sconces, direct light towards the ceiling, which reflects and spreads the light across the room. Downlights, such as recessed lights and track lights, cast light downward from the ceiling or wall. Table and floor lamps can function as both uplights and downlights by emitting light towards the ceiling and floor.

TASK LIGHTING

Task lighting provides focused illumination in smaller areas that require brighter light, such as workspaces. It should be approximately three times brighter than general lighting for optimal functionality. Using high LPW bulbs or increasing the number of fixtures can enhance general lighting. Suitable task lighting options include recessed lights, track lighting, pendants, table or floor lamps, and under-cabinet lighting strips.

ACCENT LIGHTING

Accent lighting adds brilliant shimmer to make your precious objects, paintings, sculptures, and outstanding architectural features stand out. Use a bulb that's no more than three times as bright as the surrounding general light. Position the fixture so that the light doesn't block your line of sight so that no glaring reflections bounce back.

For track lighting used in wall washing or wall grazing, direct the light beam at a 30-degree angle from the vertical to avoid glare and hot spots. Halogen lights are ideal for accent lighting due to their intensity and brilliance.

THE VISIONARY CRAFTSMANSHIP: BREATHING LIFE INTO STRUCTURES

In the illustrious realm of property development and construction, where grandeur meets precision, one name reigns supreme: L.V.D Group. This chapter unveils the intricacies of their remarkable craft, where architectural prowess and construction excellence blend seamlessly, conjuring urban wonders that defy imagination.

L.V.D Group, an embodiment of innovation, quality, and exactitude, has dedicated years to nurturing its expertise in property, development, and construction. They are not merely builders; they are sculptors who breathe life into blueprints, shaping the tomorrows that stand tall and proud. Their supremacy lies in their profound knowledge of the real estate market, and at the epicenter of this mastery, you'll find the high-end designer/architects, who add finesse to their construction marvels.

As you embark on this journey into the profound collaboration between builders who specialize in investments, developments, and construction, you'll discover that this partnership is the pulsating soul of L.V.D Group's ascent to architectural eminence.

THE UNWAVERING CRAFTSMEN: ARCHITECTS OF CONSTRUCTION

Imagine a world without these artisans, a world bereft of iconic skylines and structural marvels. These creators who stand alongside L.V.D Group are the architects of the sublime, the guardians of precision, and the designers of enduring functionality. Every project they undertake is a journey that commences with raw materials and culminates in an urban spectacle.

These artisans bear the immense responsibility of transforming visionary concepts into tangible, awe-inspiring reality. When they collaborate with L.V.D Group, their role is to craft the very core of the edifice. Their craftsmanship gives life to the architectural essence. The structures they raise mirror the integrity of the environment, the essence of the community, and the values of the client. The precision they infuse into the construction process is nothing short of symphony in stone and steel.

THE FUSION OF BRILLIANCE: VISION TRANSCENDING REALITY AND THE LEGACY: SHAPING TOMORROW

If architects are the luminaries who breathe life into these structures, then L.V.D Group's status as an icon in the construction industry hinges on the vision and creativity of their architects. They paint the canvas with concepts that transform into structural artistry.

The architect–builder collaboration within L.V.D Group is a dynamic blend of the creative and the pragmatic. Architects and designers are deeply embedded in the project from inception, ensuring that the architectural vision remains as vivacious as the day it was conceived. This unique approach ensures that the essence of the original design shines through the layers of construction.

The relationship between architects and builders at L.V.D Group is not just a transaction but a harmonious synergy. They share a common language of creation and execution. Their collaboration is the wellspring of innovative solutions and cutting-edge design. Together, they weave a tapestry of aesthetic and pragmatic marvels, enhancing the beauty and functionality of the structures they craft. In the high-end world of property development, L.V.D Group stands as an enduring symbol of success, where their construction prowess is celebrated and unrivaled. While architects contribute to the creative vision, these artisans are the architects of the urban landscape, working hand in hand to mold the tapestry of our architectural dreams.

WALLPAPER AND WALL COVERINGS

Wall coverings refer to anything used to design and dress your walls; from wallpaper and paint to more creative materials like plaster or decorative fabrics. Your choice of wall coverings should depend on the room function, your interior design vision, practical questions like maintenance, ease of installation, and your ability to change your wall covering or its color when need be.

If you plan to redesign your home interiors, modern interior design trends in wall coverings will help to choose stylish wall design ideas for your home and create beautiful and interesting rooms. Modern interior design trends can give you great inspirations to apply creative wall coverings and transform empty walls into gorgeous decorative accents for modern interior design.

Experimenting and enjoying innovative ideas, contemporary technologies, and new materials is all part of the fun that comes with creating amazing wall coverings that define modern interior design trends. Unconventional wall designs challenge traditional interior design and decor, adding unusual wall coverings and material combinations to home interiors and offices, while still creating an atmosphere of comfort.

Modern interior design trends feature nature-inspired wall coverings with digital photo prints, wood, brick, or concrete mimicking wallpaper patterns, carved wood wall paneling, floral wallpaper, geometric or striped designs, natural materials, luxurious 3D wall panels, textured wall tiles, and chic wall covering fabrics. These trends bring nature, texture, and visual interest to modern interiors.

Photo print wallpapers showcase landscapes, seascapes, and cityscapes, creating dramatic effects. Wood, brick, or concrete wallpapers add simplicity and a contemporary feel. Accent walls with wallpaper patterns and wooden paneling add depth and unique texture. Nature-inspired, floral, and landscape wallpapers blend the outdoors with interior design. Advanced technology creates realistic photo print wallpapers, integrating nature into modern spaces.

NATURAL MATERIALS

Wood, brick, concrete, or stone wall designs are a captivating blend of traditional and contemporary aesthetics. These materials serve as modern interior design trends, mimicking antique, industrial, or rustic walls and adding a striking accent to your space.

MODERN INTERIOR DESIGN TRENDS IN WALL PANELING AND TILES

Modern wall tiles that look like wood or brick are absolutely amazing. This decorative wall paneling, with decorative bricks, add a unique look to modern interior design in a vintage style blending simple and traditional into contemporary home decor.

MODERN INTERIOR DESIGN TRENDS IN TEXTURED WALL COVERINGS

3D wallpaper patterns, carved wood wall paneling, and lincrusta bring beautiful materials, various textures and geometric, striped or floral decoration patterns into modern interior design creating fabulous accents walls that make a statement. 3D wall tiles and textured wall coverings, carved wood wall paneling and luxurious wall covering fabrics, lincrusta wallpaper and painting ideas allow to create top notch rooms unleashing your imagination and offering numerous ways to not only personalize modern interior design ideas but also give them a contemporary look.

FLOORING

Hard floors have stood the test of time and continue to be favored by homeowners for their durability and aesthetic appeal. The availability of laminated timber finishes, such as water-resistant MDF, has only strengthened their popularity in the Australian market.

When it comes to floor coverings, rugs reign supreme as a versatile and practical choice. Apart from adding a touch of visual interest, floor rugs offer the added benefits of reducing noise levels and creating a cozy atmosphere. From intricately handcrafted Tibetan rugs, showcasing rich ethnic influences, to contemporary options like large squares of skins, there is a wide range of styles to suit diverse interior preferences. While dark stained floors remain a timeless classic, the abundance of timber finish options has expanded, providing homeowners with greater flexibility. This enables them to explore different finishes that align perfectly with their personal tastes and complement their overall interior design.

My Favorite Flooring.. Yes, you're seeing right. This is 3D Epoxy Flooring That Looks Oh So Real...

GARDEN VIEWS

Integrating garden and outdoor views within the interior space enhances the overall living experience, creating a harmonious connection with nature. By using large windows, glass walls, indoor plants, and natural materials, you can transform your interior into a serene and inviting sanctuary that seamlessly merges with the beauty of the outdoors.

Bringing garden and outdoor views into the interior space can create a seamless connection with nature and infuse the indoors with a refreshing and calming ambiance. Here are some design strategies to achieve this.

LARGE WINDOWS AND GLASS DOORS

Install large windows and glass doors that offer unobstructed views of the garden and outdoor surroundings. Floor-to-ceiling windows or sliding glass doors can visually extend the interior space and create a feeling of openness and integration with nature.

STRATEGIC PLACEMENT OF WINDOWS

If the architecture of your space allows, strategically position windows to frame specific garden views or focal points, such as a beautifully landscaped area, a water feature, or a striking tree. This ensures that these views become natural works of art within your interior.

OUTDOOR SEATING AREAS

If possible, design an outdoor seating area adjacent to the interior space. This creates a seamless transition between indoors and outdoors, providing opportunities to enjoy the garden views while relaxing or entertaining.

USE OF GLASS WALLS

Consider incorporating glass walls or partitions to separate interior spaces while maintaining a visual connection with the outdoors. Glass walls can be used in spaces like home offices, sunrooms, or conservatories, providing a sense of transparency and openness.

ATRIUMS AND COURTYARDS

Introduce atriums or courtyards within the interior space, allowing for greenery and natural light to penetrate deep into the building. These features become miniature gardens, creating a delightful and refreshing atmosphere indoors.

INDOOR PLANTS AND VERTICAL GARDENS

Bring greenery inside by adding indoor plants and vertical gardens. Potted plants, hanging planters, and living walls not only enhance the visual appeal of the interior but also improve indoor air quality and create a connection with nature.

REFLECTIVE SURFACES

Use mirrors and other reflective surfaces strategically to capture and multiply garden views. Placing mirrors across from windows or glass doors can effectively bring the outdoors inside, making the space feel more expansive.

NATURAL MATERIALS AND COLORS

Incorporate natural materials and earthy colors in your interior design to evoke a sense of being outdoors. Wood, stone, and natural textiles create a harmonious link between the interior and the surrounding landscape.

THE GREAT OUTDOORS
IDEAS ON DESIGNING YOUR OUTDOOR LIVING SPACE

INVENTIVE LIGHTING

To enhance your outdoor space at night, you'll need outdoor lighting. Choose creative options like ambiance lighting placed under seating or garden features. Opt for versatile and fresh lighting options that allow you to change the color at will, instantly altering the mood and ambiance of your outdoor area. This will create an appealing outdoor escape and encourage you to spend more time outside.

OUTDOOR SAUNAS

Investing in an outdoor sauna can be a valuable addition to your home. It offers a unique and relaxing experience, which can help you unwind after a long day. An outdoor sauna is a cost-effective investment that can increase the saleability and value of your property. The demand for outdoor saunas is growing, making it a popular trend in 2014. Adding this feature to your home is sure to impress visitors and potential buyers, contributing to a positive impression of your property.

USING NATURAL MATERIALS IN THE GARDEN

There is no place in the home that is more appropriate for the use of natural materials than the garden. Slabs of stone work excellently as benches and will last forever. Go for wood and stone over man-made materials such as plastic. Natural options tend to be more expensive, but if you were to calculate life to cost value, a natural stone option ends up winning.

SUNKEN SITTING IN THE POOL

Look past the stunning views and the infinity edge of the pool below and focus on the sunken seating. This is architecture and design at its finest. It looks good, plain and simple, and it's sure to impress the guests. We're been seeing a real growth in sunken seating over the past few years and it looks like this explosion is continuing in 2014 as all the pool suppliers we've seen are brandishing all types of different, creative sunken seating solutions.

FIRE PITS/FIREPLACES

It doesn't matter where you are in the world; a fire pit looks fabulous and very practical. The warmth it gives is an outside enabler, giving people the opportunity to use their garden when it's cold outside. One of the biggest factors for not using an outdoor area is either the cold or the wet; a fire pit solves one of these pickles. Wouldn't you like to spend more evening with your loved one, gazing up at the stars in front of a nice, bone warming fire? It's like sitting around a camp fire, and all the wonderful memories that come with it.

WALL GARDENS

This is especially popular, obviously, amongst home owners who have limited outdoor space or no space at all, but it's also used by home owners who want to add a splash of natural color to their wall. Succulents work especially well in wall gardens and are easy to maintain. Be creative; design a wall garden in all kinds of different shapes, sizes and colors.

This is a perfect solution for apartment owners who have green fingers but don't have a garden. A wonderful growing trend is Indoor wall gardens, especially in the bathroom are also a trend.

THE GREAT OUTDOORS
IDEAS ON DESIGNING YOUR OUTDOOR LIVING SPACE

HERB GARDENS

This is an obvious one; and it's made our list because it's still a monster of a trend. Herb gardens are especially popular amongst those who appreciate the culinary arts and those who like to know where their food is coming from. For those of you who have your own herb garden, you'll know that there's nothing quite like taking a sprig off a home grown herb and adding it to a dish you're preparing. Incredibly rewarding.

REDUCED LAWN

We've noticed this trend developing over the past decade, where people are reducing the size of their lawn and are preferring featured gardens, patios and other non-grassy areas. Great expanses of grass are great if you have children as they can play all their games uninhibited, but let's be honest, most of us don't keep our grass looking perfectly cut, green and lush to warrant having a lot of it.

SYNTHETIC LAWN

Synthetic lawn, once met with skepticism, has gained popularity as manufacturing techniques improved. It offers a low-maintenance solution for those who desire an evergreen, well-manicured appearance without the hassle of regular mowing. Synthetic grass is particularly useful in challenging growing conditions and can be easily shaped to create precise designs. While some may prefer natural grass, synthetic options provide a convenient alternative that is expected to continue growing in popularity.

People are reducing the size of their lawn and are preferring featured gardens and patios

DEKTON ONIRIKA AWAKE

ETERNAL ET NOIR

COMMON ARCHITECTURAL STYLES

AESTHETIC MOVEMENT

More of a late nineteenth-century philosophy than a real movement, this was inspired by the new cult of the Japanese aesthetic and by the Queen Anne revival. It prevailed only in England and America, with no counterpart in Europe. The emphasis was on maximum light, comfort and informality, with pale, quiet colors. Japanese symbols were a particular feature, as well as stylized sun flowers, lilies and peacocks.

AMERICAN COLONIAL

See COLONIAL (AMERICAN).

AMERICAN COUNTRY

A broad style not related to a particular period. Hallmarks include primitive furniture in sun-washed barn reds and dusty blues, stenciled motifs, patchwork, rag rugs, painted floorboards, floor cloths and match-board wainscoting.

AMERICAN EMPIRE

See EMPIRE (AMERICAN).

AMERICAN SOUTH-WEST

Spanish and Native American influences on American Colonial style; sometimes called Santa Fe style. Hallmarks include adobe walls, rough-hewn furniture, Navajo rugs and other brightly colored Native American textile designs.

ART DECO

Art Deco was a popular style from before World War I until the 1930s, drawing inspiration from primitive art, Russian Ballet, and Egyptian aesthetics. It featured geometric forms, vibrant colors, luxurious materials, and a celebration of modernity and opulence. The term "Art Deco" stands for "Arts Décoratifs" and represents various design disciplines.

ART NOUVEAU

This style was fashionable on both sides of the Atlantic from 1890 to the First World War, and is known for its sinuous lines, mainly derived from vegetal forms. Victor Horta and Henry Van de Velde in Belgium, Hector Guimard and Emile Galle in France, A H Mackmurdo and C F A Voysey in England, and Louis Sullivan and Louis C Tiffany in the United States were just a few of its gifted designers. In Scotland, Charles Rennie Mackintosh and the Glasgow School developed an influential rectilinear version inspired by Celtic ornament.

ARTS AND CRAFTS MOVEMENT

A nineteenth-century movement led by William Morris and C R Ashbee in Britain. The aim was to eschew mass-production methods and return to individually crafted furnishings of the past. Though it was meant to be an egalitarian movement, its products were too expensive for the 'masses' to buy. However, Morris's papers and fabrics were copied by manufacturers like Sanderson and Liberty, who have been reproducing them ever since. In the United States, the movement centered around the MISSION style and also the PRAIRIE SCHOOL.

BAUHAUS

Twentieth-century German school of design, an extension of the Weimar School of Arts and Crafts. Founded in 1919 by Walter Gropius, it was the most powerful single in influence in the development – and acceptance – of modern design. In 1925, the Bauhaus School moved from Weimar to Dessau, and the new office Gropius designed became a model for the contemporary dateless look that was the epitome of the INTERNATIONAL STYLE for decades after. Most of the school's principals moved to the United States at the onset of Nazi rule.

BAROQUE

Opulent, grand, ornate, seventeenth-century style that evolved from RENAISSANCE CLASSICISM. It has beendescribed as a piling up of decorative motifs into an unashamedly theatrical composition whether on canvas, brick orstone. It was used with handsome results all over Britain and Europe and in Central South America as well.

ART NOUVEAU

ARTS AND CRAFTS MOVEMENT

AESTHETIC MOVEMENT

AMERICAN COLONIAL STYLE

AMERICAN SOUTH-WEST STYLE

BEAUX ARTS

Late nineteenth-/early twentieth century American equivalent to the RENAISSANCE REVIVAL style popular in Europe and Britain at much the same time. It was named after the Ecole Des Beaux Arts in Paris, where many of its architectural exponents had trained. With the rapid growth of wealth in the United States, a great many new mansions were built based on French chateaux, Italian palazzo, TUDOR, ELIZABETHAN and JACOBEAN manor houses. Beaux Arts architects combined modern technology and its creature comforts with historically derived details, such as acanthus leaves twisting around electric light switch plates, and dolphin's feet on bathtubs. Colors and details were rich and exotic, with lavish plasterwork, beautiful joinery, panelling and gilding, as well as much much Japanese influence.

BELLE ÉPOQUE

French term for the opulent and glamorous period at the turn of the nineteenth-century and the beginning of the twentieth when, for the rich, all seemed 'sweetness and light' before the onset of the First World War.

BIEDERMEIER

An Austrian and German (and contemporaneously Scandinavian) decorative style, popular from the 1820s to the 1840s, often known as 'the poor man's EMPIRE'. It's simple, graceful furniture, mostly in golden hued wood with ebony or black stained ornamentation, remains popular today.

CHINOISERIE

European imitations of oriental decoration, furniture and decorative objects. The 'Chinese taste' for Chinese silks, porcelains, lacquer work, hand painted wallpapers and other items from Japan and India swept Europe and the United States in the eighteenth century after trade had begun with China. The demand was so high that European companies started making pseudo-oriental imitations or Chinoiseries.

CLASSICAL

Classicism is a style influenced by ancient Greek and Roman art and architecture, revived during the Italian Renaissance. It emphasizes elegance, restraint, symmetry and clean lines. Classicism incorporates Classical architectural elements like columns and pilasters, as well as motifs such as laurel wreaths and acanthus leaves. It shares similarities with Neoclassical design.

CLASSICAL ORDERS

The styles of CLASSICAL architecture - Doric, Ionic, Corinthian, Tuscan, and Composite - appeared in that order. They are based on the proportions and decoration of different column styles. In Classical architecture, even the proportions of wall sections could be derived from those of a column. The design styles often follow a cycle of Doric (simple lines), Ionic (more ornamental), and Corinthian (highly ornamental), reflecting the flow of design styles repeatedly.

COLONIAL

Colonial style evokes the nineteenth-century colonial experience in hot climates with verandas, white painted weather boarding, clapboard, handsome porticos and pillars, shutters, mosquito nets, slatted furniture, rattan, muslin and bare floor boards.

COLONIAL (AMERICAN)

This covers the early 1600s (when the early settlers had to make do with furniture that was primitive or imported) and the late eighteenth century when the federal government was established.

COLONIAL REVIVAL

Highly popular 1880s (also 1930s) American style, mixing the painted wood paneling, stenciling, and so on, of AMERICAN COUNTRY, with the fluted pilasters, Windsorchairs, etc, of early FEDERAL style.

COUNTRY STYLE

See AMERICAN COUNTRY, ENGLISH COUNTRY and FRENCH COUNTRY. Contemporary: In interior design, this means 'of today', with current furnishings, colors and mixtures.

CROMWELLIAN

The period of the Commonwealth in England (1649–1660), when Oliver Cromwell was Lord Protector of England, prior to the RESTORATION of the monarchy. It was arather stagnant time for architecture, decoration & furniture.

BEAUX ARTS

BELLE ÉPOQUE

COLONIAL STYLE

COUNTRY STYLE HOME

DE STIJL

The name for a group of avant-garde Dutch designers in the 1920s who worked only in right angles and primary colors. Members of the group included painter Piet Mondrian and the furniture designer Gerrit Rietveld. Rietveld's architectural masterpiece was the Schroder House in Utrecht. With its clean-cut surfaces and metal framed windows in continuous strips running up toa ceiling devoid of moldings, this was one ofthe model interiors for the INTERNATIONAL STYLE.

DIRECTOIRE

French style, from the last five years of the eighteenth century, between the assassination of Louis XVIduring the French Revolution and the coupd'etat of Napoleon Bonaparte. This was a simplified version of the last part of the LOUIS SEIZE style. The designs were elegant and simple, though the materials were of inferior quality to previous decades.

ECLECTIC

A combination of any number of styles and periods which, for this reason, is generally more idiosyncratic and interesting that anyone style. The nineteenth century was aperiod of rampant eclecticism, when anumber of style revivals co-existed.

EDWARDIAN

The period between the 1890s and the First World War. Design was much lighter and airier that the Victorian decoration that had gone before. The period encompassed the AESTHETIC MOVEMENT, ARTS AND CRAFTS MOVEMENT, ART NOUVEAU and the QUEENANNE REVIVAL.

ELIZABETHAN

Style during the reign of Elizabeth 1 of England in the second half of the sixteenth century. The period was one of great British prosperity so there was an increased demand for more luxurious buildings and furniture. The style was largely based on the Renaissance as translated by the French and Flemish, so was actually quite idiosyncratic, with much carving and inlay. CLASSICAL architecture orders were used, though rarely in the proper proportions. Small wood panels were combined with pilasters and columns. In low-ceilinge drooms, the paneling generally rose from the skirting to a primitive cornice.

In granderhomes, an oak dado was surmounted by amolding, then paneling and finally an entablature. Flooring downstairs was most often flagstones or slates, and upstairs it was random-width oak planks.

EMPIRE (AMERICAN)

The slightly more subdued American version of the French EMPIRE and English REGENCY styles appeared in the early part of the nineteenth-century. Inspired by Greek, Roman and Egyptian sources, the style encompassed many NEOCLASSICAL motifs together with lion's paw feet, sphinxes and Egyptian motifs, as well as the American Bald Eagle. Light cream or white woodwork was generally offset by red, green, blue or yellow walls, or by European hand-blocked wallpapers with all-overpatterns or scenic views. Either way, these backgrounds provided good foils for the mahogany furniture, gilt mirror frames and details.

EMPIRE (FRENCH)

The Empire style was a French style of the early nineteenth century. Named for France's First Empire, it includes the Consulate (1799-1804) as well as the reign of Napoleon 1 (1804- 1815).

Sometimes the reigns of Louis XVIII (1812-1824) and CharlesX (1824-1830) – France's Restoration period – are also included. Motifs were strongly in influenced by the discoveries of the ruins of Herculaneum and Pompeii, and Napoleon's Egyptian Campaigns, hence the plethora of ancient Greek, Roman and Egyptian motifs. Colors included Empire green, Empire ruby, lemon yellow, azure blue, amethyst and pearl grey, all mixed with gold and white.

ENGLISH COUNTRY

A broad, general style for which 'shabbychic' and 'faded elegance' are good descriptions. It is characterized by comfort, mellow colors and slightly faded chintzes, rugs and needle work cushions.

ETRUSCAN

A decorative style based on Roman antiquity & Etruscan ornaments. ROBERTADAM used many Etruscan motifs and ideas in his houses and, in turn, influenced the French, who called it le style Etrusque and used it greatly in the late eighteenth century.

ELIZABETHAN

COUNTRY STYLE

EDWARDIAN

NEOCLASSICAL INTERIOR

FEDERAL

The term used to describe American architecture and design from the 1780s until the early nineteenth century and based on NEOCLASSICAL. Highly prized in the United States, the style drew upon the designs of Sheraton and Hepplewhite, the early REGENCY in Britain and the early EMPIRE in France. It used most of the familiar NEOCLASSICAL motifs plus the American bald eagle as a symbol of the new federal government. Furniture was mainly mahogany or painted wood, and rooms reflected the abundance of new fabrics and French wallpapers then available in the country.

FRENCH COUNTRY

Also known as Provençal or French provincial, this style is characterised by Provençal print fabrics; sunny colour schemes of bright yellows, blues, pinks and reds; white-washed or colour washed walls in soft tones of ochre, honey, rose, apricot and russet; terracotta-tiled floors; and large solid, unfussy furniture in pine or chestnut, consisting of rustic, simplified versions of both LOUIS QUINZE and LOUIS SEIZE designs.

GEORGIAN

A term applied to British architecture and design during the reigns of George I, II, III and IV – i.e., from 1714 to 1830 – a long period which went virtually from the PALLADIAN REVIVAL to the REGENCY. Sometimes called the 'age of elegance', it was the golden age of British design in every field.

GOTHIC

A predominate style of ecclesiastical architecture in Europe during the middle ages. The Gothic style was much in favour in the eighteenth century as an antidote to rigorous CLASSICISM (when it was often spelt 'Gothick'). It was enormously popular again in the nineteenth century, when it was called Neo-Gothic or the Gothic revival and was part of a reverence by the ARTS AND CRAFTS movement for French Country Interior 50 all things medieval. The revival interpreted it more seriously. Gothic decoration includes pointed arches, tracery, ogees, and medieval motifs such as the trefoil and quatrefoil.

GRAND TOUR

An almost obligatory part of the education for rich young men in the eighteenth and nineteenth centuries, particularly the British, who became known in Italy as milordi. They flocked to Italy, Greece and, to a lesser extent France, to steep themselves in classical antiquity. After twoor three years of travelling, they returned with antiquities, furniture, sculptures, paintings and ideas on architecture, which greatly influenced the public taste.

GREEK REVIVAL

An architectural movement that developed within the NEOCLASSICAL style stressing Greek and RENAISSANCE styles. It was at its height in Britain in the 1790s and, in the1820-40s, it became equally popular in the United States, where it influenced many houses built at the time as well as much furniture design. It was also popular in Europe, particularly Germany. Staircases became much lighter than previously, with splendid stair rails. Painted, papered and fabric-covered walls replaced wood paneling and were accompanied by handsome plaster cornices and beautiful mantel pieces.

GUSTAVIAN

A charming late eighteenth-century Swedish period-style, inspired by Gustav III of Sweden, emerged in the late 18th century. Light-filled rooms featured large windows, chandeliers, and mirrors. Walls were adorned with painted panels, swags, columns, and flowers. Furniture showcased simplified Neoclassical designs and understated elegance. Cool colors like blue-grey and straw yellow, along with checked fabrics and tiled stoves, characterized the Gustavian aesthetic.

HIGH-TECH

Also spelt hi-tech, this 1980s style was based on industrial components such as stainless steel and rubber flooring with a dash of MINIMALISM and often featured bold, primary colors.

INTERNATIONAL STYLE

Also known as Modernism, launched by the BAUHAUS in the early 1920s. It advocated sleek lines, simplicity, natural textures and pale, neutral colors. Walter Gropius, Le Corbusier and Ludwig Mies van der Rohe were founder members of a style that has profoundly influenced designers up to the present day.

GOTHIC STYLE

HI-TECH

GREEK REVIVAL

GEORGIAN

JACOBEAN ARCHITECTURE

GREEK REVIVAL ARCHITECTURE

JACOBEAN

The Jacobean style refers to the architectural and design period during the reign of King James I of England in the early seventeenth century. It can be seen as amore elaborate version of the preceding Elizabethan style, incorporating new ideas and proportions inspired by the Palladian Classicism of the Italian Renaissance. During this period, a better understanding and more accurate interpretation of Palladian Classicism influenced the design aesthetic of the time.

LOUIS QUATORZE

France reached the pinnacle of aesthetic splendor during the reign of Louis XIV, embracing the opulent grandeur of Baroque style. Luxurious interiors prevailed from the late 17th to the early 19th century, led by France. These interiors boasted rich materials like velvet, serge, and damask, along with embossed leather adorned with foil, silver, or gold. Intricately carved and gilded paneling (boiserie), marble or parquet floors with Savonnerie carpets, and lavish gilt-bronze chandeliers, clocks & decorative objects further defined the French aesthetic during this period.

LOUIS QUINZE

The French version of ROCOCO, which reaches its height during the reign of Louis XV (1715-1774). Colors were pale pastels with cream and white. Mirrors were used lavishly. They were set over console tables; were recessed into carved and gilded panelling (boiserie) opposite tall over-mantel mirrors; and were used to disguise places in summer, as well as on ceilings and sometimes on sliding window shutters; occasionally entire walls were lined withthem. Add to this the elaborately framed hanging mirrors, the hundreds of candles set into crystal candelabra and the girandoles (candlesticks set into mirrors) and you get an idea of the dazzling effect.

LOUIS SEIZE

The NEOCLASSICAL style that swept though Europe from the 1750s was known in France as 'le gout grec'. However, it is also known simply as Louis Seize, after the reigning monarch Louis XVI (1774-1793), who presided over the full resurgence of Classicism in France. Neoclassical motifs such as caryatids, acanthus and laurelwreaths appeared on furniture.

blue cloud-painted ceilings and colors like terracotta and purple were added to the predominant gold and white, as Etruscan and Egyptian details began to beadded to the Classical repertoire.

MANNERISM

The transition between RENAISSANCE & BAROQUE movements, in which designs included strangely attenuated human figures and 'grotesque' ornament in the form of griffins, birds and insects set within cartouches connected by strap work designs. The term 'grotesque' was derived from ancient Roman decoration excavated during the Renaissance, and had its roots in the word grotto, or cave, rather than the current meaning. It was a deliberate reaction to the discipline of CLASSICISM and It was particularly popular in northern Europe in the sixteenth and seventeenth centuries.

MINIMALISM

70's, 90's and current movement which follows Ludwig Miesvan der Rohe's dictum that 'less-is-more'. All ornamentation is eschewed along with clutter and most colour creating clean-lined interiors whose success depends on the detail.

MISSION

An 1890's/early 1900's American offshoot of the ARTS AND CRAFTS movement. Its exponents, particularly the Roycroft community and Gustav Stickley, believed they had a mission to promulgate utility of design. The name is also linked with the simple furniture of the early Spanish missions in California and New Mexico. It originated when members of a San Francisco mission made chairs to replace decrepit pews.

MODERNISM

See INTERNATIONAL STYLE.

NEOCLASSICAL

The first real international style and a major design force from 1760 to 1830, emerged as a reaction against Rococo's excesses. Inspired by archaeological discoveries in ancient Greece, Rome, and Egypt, it embodied the Age of Reason. The style incorporated motifs like acanthus leaves, lyres, lion's heads, laurel wreaths, crossed spears, swan's necks, sphinxes and palmettos. Neoclassicism became an influential international style, representing a return to classical elegance and rationality.

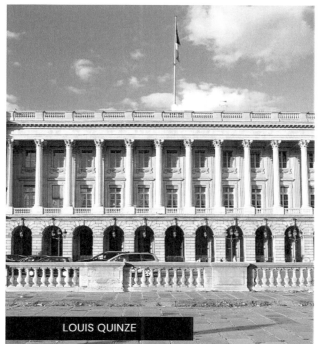

LOUIS QUINZE

NEOCLASSICAL

MANNERISM

LOUIS QUATORZE

MODERNISM STYLE

QUEEN ANNE REVIVAL STYLE

PALLADIAN AND NEO-PALLADIAN

The architectural style derived from the designs of Andrea Palladio, the great Renaissance architect known for basing his buildings on the principles of ancient classical architecture. Introduced to Britain by Inigo Jones in the seventeenth century, Palladio's pure and exquisitely proportioned designs were later revived in the early eighteenth century. It isinteresting to note that while Neo-Palladian (or Palladian revival) architecture exhibited severe geometric quality, the furniture associated with it had a more Baroque feel.This is primarily because William Kent, aprominent figure of the eighteenth century who popularized Palladio's work, did not have a direct model for ancient classical furnishings. Instead, he adapted the Baroque furniture he encountered in Palladian villas in northern Italy.

PRAIRIE SCHOOL

Designs by the American master architects Frank Lloyd Wright and Louis Sullivan and a group of other architects and designers centered around Chicago from the late 1880s to the early 1900s. Its various influences were the low, rugged, rambling ranch houses of the prairie, hence its name; the ARTS AND CRAFT MOVEMENT from Britain and it's American offshoot, MISSION.

PROVINCIAL

See FRENCH COUNTRY.

QUEEN ANNE

This gently simplified British adaptation of the BAROQUE was named for Queen Anne, who reigned from 1702 to 1714. Nothing much changed in room decoration from the WILLIAM AND MARY period preceding it, but furniture became fluid and beautiful, based on simple elegance, subtle curves and understatement. The vogue grew for CHINOISERIE and for 'chinaware', which often covered every available shelf as well as the walls. Wallpapers had a huge success with the middle classes, while the aristocracy was hanging Chinese silks. The style continued for years after the monarch's death, till it gave way to the PALLADIAN REVIVAL style.

QUEEN ANNE (AMERICAN)

In America the QUEEN ANNE style began totake hold just as it was waning in Britain (i.e., around 1720), and was influential until the middle of the eighteenth century.

QUEEN ANNE REVIVAL

The so-called Queen Anne revival at the end of the nineteenth century in Britain had very little to do with the early eighteenth century QUEEN ANNE style, and was much more a mixture of NEOCLASSICAL designs, with the odd nod to ROCOCO. It was led by the English country-house architect Richard Norman Shaw, who tried to reproduce this lightness of touch in revolt against Victorian heaviness.

REGENCY

Early eighteenth-century French style of the richly gilded interiors during the transitional period between the magnificent BAROQUE and LOUIS QUATORiZE and the full-blown ROCOCO of LOUIS QUINZE. It roughly coincided with the period when Philippe d'Orleans was regent to the young Louis XV.

REGENCY

The Regency style, named after the Prince Regent of Britain, was a late neoclassical British style that gained popularity in the first four decades of the 19th century. It incorporated a wide range of motifs from various sources including Greek, Roman, Egyptian, French, Chinese, and Hindu influences. The style featured motifs like eagles, pyramids, sphinxes, winged lions, and crossed-spears as well as striped tenting and chairs with sabrelegs. Deep colors like terracotta, maroon, or yellow were often used for painted walls, while both tented and clouded ceilings were fashionable. Curtain treatments were elaborate and multi-layered, featuring outer curtains, under curtains, muslin curtains and sun blinds, often with poles or deepvalances and intricate trimmings.

RENAISSANCE REVIVAL

Also known as Neo-Renaissance, this was amuch-favored style in the latter part of thenineteenth century. Its heavy forms andelaborate decoration were actually taken from the RENAISSANCE and the BAROQUE and marked a return of interest in the NEOCLASSICAL style.

PROVINCIAL

QUEEN ANNE

PRAIRIE SCHOOL

REGENCY

VICTORIAN ARCHITECTURE

RENAISSANCE

The Renaissance, meaning rebirth, was a significant design movement that originated in Italy during the great quattrocento, the Italian equivalent to the glorious Greek fifth century BC. It marked the first revival of the Classical style and was most prominent in the late fourteenth and fifteenth centuries in Italy, where the northern Gothic style had not gained much attraction. The Renaissance style gradually spread to France in the first half of the sixteenth century, followed by Spain, the Netherlands and Germany.

RESTORATION

The period after Charles II was restored to the British throne in 1660 following the CROMWELLIAN period. Restoration style was the first real English BAROQUE, impregnated with a sense of luxury and sumptuousness brought back by Charles from his sojourn at the grand court of Louis XIV. He imported Dutch, Flemish, Spanish and French craftsmen, but the most famous craftsman of the period was the woodcarver Grinling Gibbons. The taste forwalnut started at this time, along with thatfor gilded gesso, silver decoration and marquetry.

Panelling inspired by the boiserie at Versailles, ran from the dado to the ceiling, capped by a sophisticated cornice, with smaller, rectangular panelling set under the chair rail. Made from oak or walnut, it was left in its natural state and waxed, or was sometimes marbled. Tapestries were often hung within the larger panels. Softwoods were frequently grained to resemble the more expensive walnut or oak. Mouldings and carvings were often gilded. If panelling was not used, walls were plastered and covered with damask or velvet. Cheaper alternatives were the new wallpapers. Oriental rugs began to be usedon the parquet floors, rather than on tables. Adding to the richness were candles conces in silver, brass and iron, and the first crystal chandeliers.

ROCOCO

This movement originated in France around 1700. The style was particularly identified with the reign of Louis XV and spread all over Europe during the early eighteenth century, particularly to Germany, Austria, Spain, Scandinavia and the Netherlands. It never reached quite the same heights of popularity in Britain and America, although there were many Rococo pattern books incirculation.

A reaction to the formal heaviness of the BAROQUE, it was a light-hearted, frivolous style. Its decoration relied on shells and flowers, its forms were curved, its furniture more comfortable, it's colors pastel. Candles were reflected a hundred times by mirrors; windows were enlarged; the forms and motifs of CHINOISERIE were embraced, as well as anything to do with monkeys, often dressed up in human clothes.

ROCOCO REVIVAL

Also known as Neo-Rococo, this curvilinear, rather florid nineteenth century style startedin Britain, where French taste was once again vastly admired, in spite of the Napoleonic Wars. It was popular too in France, where it was known as le style Pompadour, during the reign of Louis-Philippe (1830-1848). It reached Germanyduring the second half of the century and from there spread to the United States.

ROCOCO SHAKER

A style loosely based on the simple, functional interiors of America's Shakersect, founded in 1774 but at their most populous in the first half of the nineteenth century.

They are best known for their beautifully crafted, clean lined wood furniture, much of it built in, their stacking oval boxes with dovetail joints and their habit of hanging chairs, brooms, mirrors, baskets, etc, on peg rails around the room to keep the floors clear. They held that' beauty rests on utility – a philosophy that was, in many ways, a precursor to the late nineteenth – and early – twentieth-century doctrine of functionalism and the American architect Louis Sullivan's famous tenet, 'form follows function'.

SANTA FE

See AMERICAN SOUTH-WEST.

TROUBADOUR

The Troubadour style emerged as a French, nineteenth-century rendition of the Neo-Gothic style, deeply influenced by the cult of medievalism. This aesthetic movement embraced Gothic ornamentation, which found its way onto furniture, tapestries, and various small objects.

RENAISSANCE

RENAISSANCE REVIVAL

ROCOCO STYLE

SANTA FE STYLE

ROCOCO SHAKER STYLE

TUDOR

Roughly the first half of the sixteenth century, this style-period covers the reign of the English Tudor monarchs; apart from the ELIZABETHAN period of Elizabeth I. Gothic forms still predominated at the beginning of the period but were being slowly diffused by the gradual introduction of ideas from the Renaissance. Pargetting (decorative plasterwork), very often richly colored and covered the ceilings with Tudor roses, scrolls, cartouches and fleurs-de-lis. Walls were generally panelled, and the field (centre) of the panel was usually carved with a linen fold design.

VICTORIAN

The umbrella title given to Queen Victoria's reign in Britain from 1837 to 1901. In fact, the name was given to most nineteenth century design all over the world during that time. It included an eclectic mixture of nostalgic revivalist styles, such as NEO-Baroque, Neo-Renaissance, NeoRococo andso on, as well as the avant-garde reactionsto this revivalism: THE ARTS AND CRAFTS MOVEMENT, THE AESTHETIC MOVEMENT and ART NOUVEAU.

WILLIAM AND MARY

This BAROQUE style, practiced in the late seventeenth century in Britain then in America, was named after the joint reign in Britain of the Dutch William III (1689-1702) and his English wife, Mary II (1689-1694). It was a more toned down style than the exuberant Restoration period that preceded it, and a precursor of the splendid early eighteenth-century QUEENANNE style. William brought with him a whole team of Dutch craftsmen, as well as promulgating his own taste for the blue-and-white porcelain being shipped from China by the Dutch East India Company.

VIENNA SECESSION

In Germany and Austria, at the beginning of the twentieth century, the newly established Vienna Secession group began designing deliberately stark buildings with integrated interiors. Walls were plain plaster, devoid of cornices and mouldings. These were the precursors to standardized mass housing.

VIENNA SECESSION

TUDOR STYLE

WILLIAM AND MARY

VICTORIAN STYLE

FURNITURE STYLES A-Z

Armoire - large, moveable cupboard with doors and shelves for storing clothing used commonly as an entertainment cabinet or for storage.

Baroque - extravagant and heavily ornate style of architecture, furniture, and decoration.

Camelback - sofa back that is irregular in the shape of a large, central hump.

Chaise - a loveseat or sofa with only one arm, the back usually doesn't reach the end of the cushion.

Daybed - seating piece that can also serve as a bed.

Faceted - decorative surface cut into sharp-edged planes in a crisscross pattern to react light

Hampton style - furniture modeled after the American Colonial Style or after the European 15th Century.

MDF - medium density finer board usually finished in paint, veneers, or laminates.

Ottoman - upholstered footstool.

Runners - strips of wood on which doors slide.

Spat - middle piece of the back support of a chair.

Wing chair - a fully upholstered chair with wings at the sides to protect sitter from drafts.

Chairs - With chairs, comfort results when weight and pressure are spread and tension is eased if seat height is slightly shorter than the sitter's lower legs, allowing for feet to rest comfortably on the floor. Similarly, the seat depth should be shorter than the sitter's upper leg to avoid any pressure points. Ample width in the seat enables freedom of movement.

Resilient shaping of the seat helps distribute pressure evenly. Both the seat and back should have a slight backward tilt to provide support. The angle between the seat and back should be at least 95 degrees. Adequate lumbar support is crucial for the small of the sitter's back. Adjustability of seat and back positions can accommodate different individuals and relaxation preferences. Additionally, lightweight yet sturdy side chairs offer flexibility in furniture arrangement and convenient floor cleaning.

Tables - When selecting a table look for:

- Necessary strength and stability.
- Supports that are out of the way of feet and legs.
- The right height, size and shape for their intended use.
- Made of durable materials.

Coffee tables – Functional coffee tables are essential for a living room. They should provide storage space for items like magazines and remote controls, be at a comfortable height, and not obstruct traffic flow. Ideally, coffee tables should be around 40cm high, incorporate storage, have a durable surface, and feature strong yet slender supports.

End tables –End tables are practical and versatile, doubling as storage with drawers and shelves. They should be lightweight yet sturdy, placed conveniently near chairs in a living area. These tables provide supplementary storage, don't obstruct feet, and can support table lamps. Ideal height aligns with furniture arms, but slight variations enhance convenience. Nests of tables simplify entertaining.

Dining Tables – Sit down meals require a table that is stable enough not to be rocked by children bumping into it or someone carving a roast on it. The top should be large enough to give each person 60cm of elbow room and high enough to give leg room between chair and lower surface. Supports should be out of the way of sitters' feet and knees.

Table surface durability and maintenance ease are important as tablecloths are less common. Rectangular tables are versatile, while round or oval tables foster a convivial atmosphere Most dining tables are rectangular, as they are harmonious with rectangular rooms, can be pushed against a wall or into a corner and are slightly less costly to make. In the right setting however, a round or oval table will give a friendly, convivial group feeling.

Always Check compatibility between chairs and table, including leg interference, coordinated heights, and comfortable spacing.

THEIKOS COLLECTIONS

Exquisite Australian made crystal designs that elevate the art of craftsmanship. From captivating crystal photo frames to an array of handcrafted stone creations, every piece is a testament to beauty and individuality.

Immerse yourself in the world of Theikos Collections, where photo frames become works of art. Meticulously crafted, each frame boasts radiant crystals that encircle the image, creating a mesmerizing contrast. With a middle part left empty, your cherished memories take center stage, while the surrounding stones add an aura of elegance.

But the magic doesn't stop there. Theikos Collections offers a diverse range of handcrafted items, each bearing the mark of artisanal excellence. Discover exquisite jewelry pieces that adorn you with the brilliance of stones. Unleash the power of stone sculptures and crystal vases, transforming your living space into a sanctuary of style.

Hand Made Crystal Design

THEIKOS COLLECTIONS

DESI
0451253523

To explore their stunning collection and learn more about the handcrafted items, you can visit Theikos Collection's Instagram page **@theikoscollections**. The Instagram page serves as a visual showcase, providing glimpses of the intricate craftsmanship and remarkable designs of their stone-based creations.

For further inquiries or to request more information about specific items, you can send direct message to Theikos Collections on Instagram.

STAGE TO SELL AND GET MORE BANG FOR YOUR BUCK

I n today's competitive Real Estate market landscape, the impact of staging on property sales is more pronounced than ever. Recent data reveals that staged homes not only command higher prices but also spend significantly less time on the market, redefining the importance of maximizing every aspect of a property to create a lasting positive impression.

Around the world the influence of effective staging can be quantified as an impressive 10% additional return for s ellers. This statistic underscores the potential financial gains that can be unlocked by preparing and styling a property for sale. By doing so, you're not merely presenting a house; you're orchestrating an emotional experience that resonates with prospective buyers, prompting them to make swift, heartfelt decisions.

Real estate broker @Claudia_Michaels, owner of CM REALTY explains, that in today's fast-paced real estate market, adopting a "SELL IT AS IS" mentality is simply not viable. Buyers may approach property shopping with logic, but ultimately, they make their decisions driven by emotion.

Astonishingly, within just 10 seconds of arriving at a property, potential buyers form their initial judgments. This emphasizes the pivotal role that presentation plays in the sales process. Staging a property for sale is a multifaceted endeavor that doesn't always necessitate acquiring new items. Instead, you can leverage your creativity and design acumen to breathe new life into a space through rearrangement, reuse, and the strategic removal of existing furniture. This not only maximizes the available space but also creates an overall impression that resonates with buyers on an emotional level.

In the realm of real estate, two factors stand tall as the guiding lights toward a successful sale: price and presentation. A well-executed presentation, with an emphasis on creating beautiful interiors, has the potential to lure in higher offers. The good news is that this process need not break the bank. With dedication and thoughtful consideration, crafting stunning interiors is an achievable goal for anyone willing to invest the effort or you can engage an interior design staging expert.

By mastering the fundamentals of interior design, you too can transform properties into captivating and market-ready homes without the need for substantial financial investments. This approach not only translates to higher selling prices and faster transactions but also fosters a deeper connection between buyers and the properties they aspire to call home. In this ever-evolving real estate landscape, preparation and presentation remain the keys to unlocking success.

INTERIOR DESIGN OR LEARNING THE ROPES FOR YOUR BUSINESS?

Interior design career opportunities are diverse and offer various paths to explore. Whether you're interested in commercial interior design, residential interior design, or other specialized areas, there are plenty of options to choose from. Building a strong rapport with clients is crucial for success, as it helps you understand their needs and create designs that meet their expectations.

In commercial interior design, projects can range from small boutique retail spaces to larger corporate or institutional projects. While independent designers or small practices can handle smaller projects, larger projects may require collaboration with specialists in certain areas, such as commercial kitchen design.

Residential design is in high demand, adding value to homes. You can establish your own consultancy within a building or property firm or work for existing design firms, specializing in areas like kitchen and bathroom design or retail sales. Explore the diverse possibilities of an interior design career today!

Unlock your creative potential with our fabulous Interior Design Course, **"Interior Design Mastery"**. This online Advanced Diploma program offers easy-to-read and comprehensive content, guiding you through the world of interior design. Join now to learn all there is to know!

Visit **www.katerina-kapellaki.com/courses** for more information.

Computer-assisted design (CAD) skills are also in demand, particularly for creating visual representations of proposed designs.
You can specialize in designing apartments, planning materials, and settings for developers.

Entrepreneurial opportunities exist for buying, renovating, and renting out properties to build a strong portfolio. Color consultancy is another avenue where you can assist clients in making bold and confident color choices for their spaces. Additionally, specializing in smart house technology, ecologically sustainable design (ESD), exhibition design, window dressing, product display, styling for photography shoots, writing for interiors publications, or marketing and public relations for design professionals are all viable career options.

The field of interior design offers a wide range of opportunities, allowing you to choose a path that aligns with your interests and skills. By honing your design and project management skills, you can create a successful career in this dynamic industry.

MONASTERY PANAGIA KALIVIANI

This place holds a special significance in my journey. It is the very orphanage where my mother spent her childhood. From a tender age of around four or five, I vividly recall my fascination with designing orphanages, which I fondly referred to as "happy homes."

An odd choice of institution for a young child to design, some may think, but for me it was all too fitting, with both my parents growing up in orphanages in Crete.

I would design my own so that other orphans would have better or more functional and spacious rooms, more sunlight, colors etc. Those drawings would inspire me to pursue what I refer to as my "life's purpose" in transforming and creating beautiful spaces for people.

This divine little church **TIMIOS STAVROS, KARTALO, GRIGORIA, CRETE** is on top of a mountain on the Island of Crete In Greece where my father helped build this just after he was old enough to leave the orphanage.

Dear Readers,

As I conclude "Design Decadence A~Ω," I thank God and my heart swells with gratitude. This book, a labor of love, celebrates my passion for interior design and architecture. I'm humbled by the support received during this creative journey. To my family, your unwavering encouragement inspired me. To the design professionals, especially Suman, whose brilliance and expertise helped bring this book to life, I am forever grateful.

And to you, dear readers, thank you! Your interest in "Design Decadence A~Ω" made every moment worthwhile. May it inspire you to embrace the beauty of design and create spaces that reflect your unique style.

With heartfelt appreciation,

Katerina Kapellaki

Milton Keynes UK
Ingram Content Group UK Ltd.
UKRC031628090224
437495UK00001BA/2

9 780975 631607